WHAT TO DO WHEN LEADERSHIP IS NEEDED

A workbook for managers of teams who aspire to become leaders.

Author of the best-selling
"What To Do When You Become The Boss"

Bob Selden
PO Box 8
Ashhurst, Palmerston North, 4470
New Zealand
ISBN 978-0-6454956-2-1 Copyright © Bob Selden 2022

National Library of Australia
Cataloguing-in-publication data:
Creator: Selden, Bob, author.
Title: What To Do When Leadership Is Needed: A workbook for managers of teams who aspire to become leaders / Bob Selden.
ISBN: 978-0-6454956-2-1(paperback)
Notes: Includes bibliographical references.

Subjects:
Leadership.
Manager as Leader.
Business and Economics.
Education.
Self Help.
Dewey Number: 331

Cover design by: Ben Odering

Other titles by Bob Selden:

What To Do When You Become The Boss:
How new managers become successful managers

Don't:
How using the right words will change your life

Setting the Tone from the Top:
How director conversations shape culture
(with Dr. Melinda Muth)

WHAT TO DO WHEN LEADERSHIP IS NEEDED

A workbook for managers of teams
who aspire to become leaders.

BOB SELDEN

Author of the best-selling *"What To Do When You Become The Boss"*

Organisations appoint people to be accountable for the performance of others – they give these people the title of 'manager'.

Then, when the manager's team members believe in and trust the manager, their team members call their managers 'leaders'.

This subtle, yet imperative difference of how titles are acquired, is the underpinning theme of this workbook.

AND SO THE STORY BEGINS ...

Travelling on a plane (pre-Covid), we taxied into the terminal and as usual when the 'Fasten seat belt' signs went off, everyone started getting their personal luggage ready for disembarking. Then also as usual, we waited.

Standing in the aisle behind a mother with two young children, aged about four and five, I heard the little four year old girl ask her mother, "Mummy, what's behind that curtain?"

The mother replied, "They're Business Class people behind that curtain".

To which the little girl responded, "Mummy, are Business Class people learners?"

Now, I've no idea of how or why that little girl put the concept of 'learning' together with 'Business Class people', but her question started me thinking about how we learn, and in particular, how people learn to become leaders.

Whilst the 'nature-nurture' debate about how people develop as leaders has raged for decades, there is an increasing body of evidence to suggest that to at least some extent, leaders are made not born. My belief is the nurture component of leadership development comes about through the stories we hear and read; how we interpret these stories and the elements from them that we choose to internalise.

Gradually over time as we hear more stories, we subconsciously build our own model of leadership.

As Warren Bennis, the leading leadership researcher and author suggests, "One cannot be taught to become a leader but one can learn to become a leader over the years through life and work experiences; through mentors and personal reflection".

This book is about some of the events I've seen, heard or experienced and that have particular leadership relevance for me. I've written about them as stories in the hope that they will resonate with you and also perhaps remind you of some stories that have influenced your development as a leader. Ultimately, I'd like to think that through reading and reflecting on these stories (and your own), you'll be able to develop and recognise fully your own, individual model of leadership.

In using stories as a learning tool, I'm heartened by author Paul Smith who comments in *Lead With A Story,* "Everybody – regardless of age, race, or gender – likes to listen to stories ... learning derived from a well-told story is remembered more accurately and for far longer than the learning derived from facts and figures."

What To Do When Leadership Is Needed has been designed as a workbook for people who lead teams – each story can be used as the basis for making your team meetings interesting, memorable and most importantly, relevant, or as a trigger as to how your own stories could be used as a key team leadership tool for both yourself and your team.

I trust you enjoy reading my stories as much as I enjoyed writing them. However, there is a caveat to using this book. Let me explain ...

One way of describing one's management style is to ask, "Is your style more one of consensus, particularly when making decisions that may affect your team, or could your style be described more as directive?" Look at the following continuum. Plot yourself along the continuum where you feel most comfortable when making decisions in your current role ...

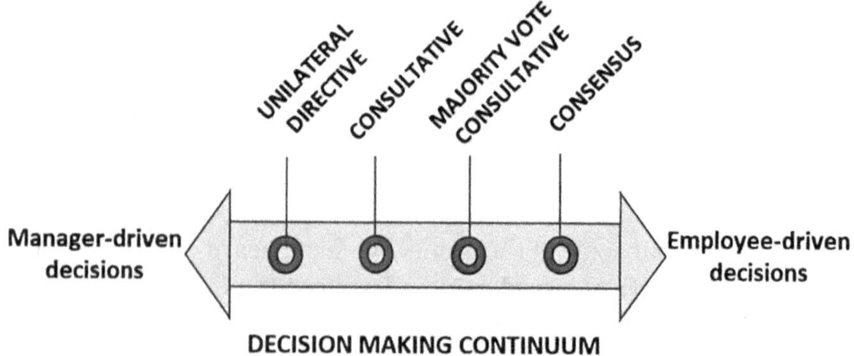

Now, as I've said in my previous book, *What To Do When You Become The Boss: How new managers become successful managers*, all styles can be effective depending on the situation.

What To Do When Leadership Is Needed is intended for managers whose style is closer to the consensus end of the continuum and who have the opportunity to use a consensus based decision making style most often. If your natural style is further toward the directive end of the continuum, or you work in an organisation where authority, title and position are key drivers of success, then this book is not for you. In fact, should you start using a more consensus style in such an organisation, it may become a career limiting move (unless you are purposely working as an agent of change).

And one other thing I should point out – because the meeting process recommended here is closer to the consensus end of the continuum, these meetings will take longer than perhaps your normal meeting takes. The payoff is a far greater degree of commitment to the decisions made within the team.

Please keep these points in mind before proceeding.

CONTENTS

Introduction: Let's get started on Leadership!

We all like to hear stories, even when they are sometimes confronting – it's the best and most interesting way of communicating. Once someone starts to tell a story, the listeners all start imagining and visualising what is happening, what's about to happen, and what's the point of the story. And the better the storyteller, the more involved the listeners become in the story.

For example, in the London riots of August 2011, you may recall the terrible video footage of Malaysian student Asyraf Haziq being attacked and robbed. As Haziq lay dazed on the footpath, his attackers first pretended to help him; then helped themselves to his belongings from his backpack, and finally ran away.

This video was shown again and again during the riots as an example of the mob culture that had developed in many parts of London at that time.

As Asyraf Haziq sat modestly dabbing his broken jaw with a small cloth during a press conference after leaving hospital, he was asked "How do you feel now about your attackers?" Haziq's response – "I feel sorry for them. It was very sad. They were so young."

Whether you saw this video clip or not, I'm sure you now have a visual image of the event and a feeling for the way Asyraf Haziq handled himself during that interview.

Now, what's the leadership message in this story? What can we learn from Asyraf Haziq's display of humility and forgiveness?

Quite often we learn something new from a story, or perhaps confirm something that we already knew. Other stories get us questioning our own thoughts and beliefs about the subject. Or perhaps others put a point of view with which we strongly disagree.

Whatever the case, the involving nature of a story is one good way of learning. Often this learning is subconscious. Rarely do we sit back after hearing a story and say, "What did I learn from that?"

How do you think Asyraf Haziq's display of humility and forgiveness relate to leadership? Is there something you personally can take from this story?

Stories - the four key questions on learning about leadership

What To Do When Leadership Is Needed, is about how we as managers of teams can learn about leadership from stories, particularly those about current events and how we can best use these in team development. Importantly, it's about how to analyse the 'standout' current events and make this story link to your team's development and perhaps even to yours and other's personal leadership development.

Suggested questions for learning from events and stories:

1. What went well or not so well in this event?

2. What can I learn as a leader from this event?

3. What would I (or my organization, my team) do differently in similar circumstances?

4. Is there something I now need to plan for as a result of this learning? If so, what?

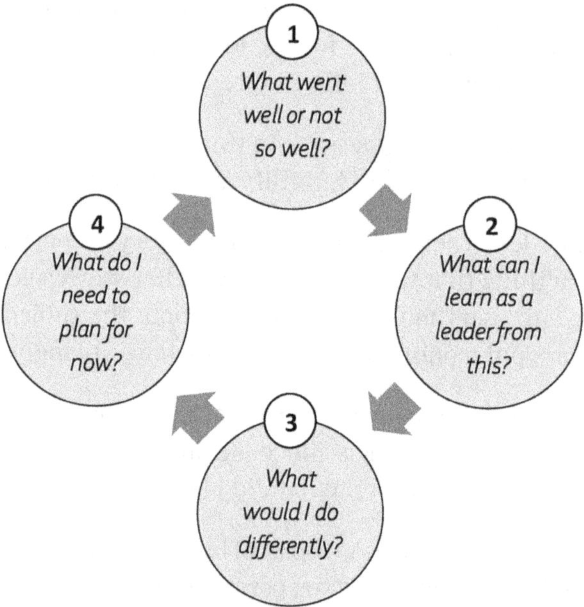

WHAT TO DO WHEN LEADERSHIP IS NEEDED

Stories, teams, leadership and you!

By its very nature, leadership requires followers. So, rather than focus predominately on developing some of the personal leadership traits, behaviours, styles etc., covered in many other leadership books, I've chosen to focus on your role in managing teams – the people who will follow you if they perceive you as a good leader. My hope with this approach is that in the process of working with your team, you'll also discover some of the key elements about your own leadership methods, style and behaviour, and why they are working for you.

There are no prescriptive answers here – rather I'm suggesting a process of learning about leadership through working with your team. However, what I can say is that working with many people whom I've observed over the last 30 years to be leaders, they develop as leaders because they do four things for those they work with or influence:

1. **They help us understand and make sense of our environment.** So for example, when things aren't working out or are unclear for us, they are able to explain what is happening in practical terms that we can understand.

2. **They help give us a sense of direction.** They are able to paint a picture of a brighter future and help us believe that we can achieve the things we want to achieve.

3. **They give us a belief in the values that are important to us.** In doing so, they make us feel part of a team of people that share these values and have the same aims.

4. **They are able to make us feel powerful** by allowing us the freedom to make decisions about our life, work and the future.

As you read or use some of the stories in *What To Do When Leadership Is Needed* either for your own leadership development, or for that of your team or group, you may care to ask yourself:

How can I provide or develop with my people . . .
- a shared understanding of *the environment?*
- a shared *vision* of where we are going?
- a shared set of *organisational values?*
- a shared *feeling of power?*

Doing so will greatly enhance your leadership aspirations.

Team and Individual Learning: a call to action at the conclusion of each story

Over the last two decades or so, I've written a number of stories about situations that struck a chord with me. These stories illustrate points which I've been making over the years I've been involved with leadership research and with helping managers develop as better managers and ultimately, leaders.

The 27 stories I've selected for this book are ones that I feel are particularly relevant for managers and their development as team leaders. Each story follows a three-step process.

1. Personal leadership review and learning

Firstly, at the end of each story, there's a series of questions to get you thinking about what you can glean as a leader from the event. This series of questions is in fact the four that are mentioned above with perhaps a slight twist to suit the story. The idea is to become familiar and comfortable with this 'four-question' process of personal enquiry, so that you will consciously apply it as a learning tool every time you read, see or hear about a new news story that is of interest to you.

2. Author's note

For some stories, I've added a postscript that describes events following the original one, or I've made an observation which could be useful for your leadership development in relation to this story.

3. Team learning exercise

Following each story there are suggestions for team activities that you can use in the workplace as a further means of leadership

     WHAT TO DO WHEN LEADERSHIP IS NEEDED

enquiry and learning based on this particular event. Some stories are ancient (for example, although first written in 2008, Plato gets a mention in my second story), some are more recent, and some are timeless!

Each team learning exercise is designed to suit the story, although they all follow a similar format. This format is one that I've used all over the world to suit varying teams – sports teams, production line and farm worker teams, social and health professionals' teams, management teams, corporate boards and government committees. The format is tried and tested across all types of teams.

This team learning exercise is a format that you can use with your group or team on a regular basis to analyse and learn from any event or story you come across that may be of interest to you, your team or your organisation.

About the stories ...

At this point, I should explain how I came to write each of these 27 stories. You'll see that some are from business, some from sport, some from community events and so on. Also, you'll notice that some have very positive outcomes, whilst others have negative consequences (at least for the participants).

Whilst I've written many articles and a number of books since the Global Financial Crisis (GFC) of 2008, the GFC and its resultant aftermath on organisations, fascinates me (even more so now that we can compare it with the results of Covid-19). After World War II, many of the great psychological theories around such things as individual motivation were discovered, researched and penned. In times of personal struggle and devastation brought on by war or natural disasters, people behave often quite differently to the way they might in normal times. So following WWII in the decades of the 1950's, '60's and '70's, psychologists took major strides towards understanding human behaviour - perhaps more so than at any time in our history.

My fascination with the GFC and the years since, is somewhat similar – I believe that organisations, like people, 'behave' quite differently in times of stress and impending crises. And so, you'll find a number of the stories in What To Do When Leadership Is Needed, were originally written at the time of the GFC or shortly thereafter. Where appropriate, I've added a postscript to some stories – with others you may care to consider your own postscript based on your learnings or understanding – I hope you do add the odd PS or two, as this workbook is aimed at managers developing their own theories of leadership.

I also believe that the organisational crisis of the GFC, and more recently Covid- 19, have given us ideal opportunities to study how organisations and people, behave and adapt in uncertain times. The Covid 19 Pandemic for instance, whilst a devastating phenomenon, can provide some excellent learning for organisations and managers. For cxample the shift to work from home, or hybrid home/workplace working as a result of lockdowns in many countries, is but one example.

As an avid follower of the news media (traditional and social), I find myself firstly interested in certain events; then subconsciously analysing and questioning them. This process of personal enquiry has led me to ask, "What are the leadership or management issues involved in this event?" Finally, my take on the current event starts to emerge as a story that perhaps managers will also find interesting and can learn from. I trust you find my stories appealing as a learning tool too.

In editing early drafts of this book, it was interesting for me as I read back over these stories, to see some leadership trends emerging. So, you'll notice that I have grouped the stories under certain headings that could well become the beginnings of a leadership development plan for you, your team, or even your organisation (these headings are listed below, so if you have an immediate need to do some work with your team on one of these topics, you can jump straight to that section).

I've also put these headings together in a final chapter in the book titled "Your strategic leadership plan". You may wish to use this as a road map for your own leadership journey. If you do, my suggestion is to jump straight to the Leadership Plan Template at the back of the book now to see how it's structured. Then you can take a note or two from the stories that have relevance for your leadership journey and use these when developing your Leadership Plan.

All the best with your story learning. If you've got a good leadership story, I'd love to hear from you. You can contact me via my website www.bobselden.com

Bon voyage!
Bob Selden

WHAT TO DO WHEN LEADERSHIP IS NEEDED TO...

Define the *STRUCTURE* and *ROLES* within your team

Set *STRATEGY* and *DIRECTION* for the team

Manage a team or organisation *CRISIS*

Develop *PERSONAL LEADERSHIP*

Develop *TRUST* and *CREDIBILITY* within the team

Manage all the key *STAKEHOLDERS* of your team

Build a *TEAM* or *GROUP*

MANAGE the *PEOPLE* in your team and organisation

MOTIVATE PEOPLE with effective performance management

Have your people provide great *CUSTOMER SERVICE*

Develop *CREATIVITY* within your people

COMMUNICATE to *INFLUENCE*

Develop *SELF-MANAGEMENT* within yourself and your team

THE IMPORTANCE OF *STRUCTURE* AND *ROLES* IN DEVELOPING LEADERSHIP

1. **WHO'S IN CHARGE?**
   - How to develop clear roles within the team

2. **DID PLATO HAVE THE ANSWER TO WALL STREET'S PROBLEMS?**
   - How to help people take personal responsibility
   - How to develop distributed leadership within your team

STORY 1:
14 JUNE 2010

Who's in charge?

What led to the disaster at BP's Deepwater Horizon oil rig in April 2010 — one of the greatest environmental disasters ever? It would be easy to say that it was a technical problem. True, the blowout preventer, a critical fail-safe mechanism on the ocean floor, failed. But the problem goes much deeper than that (excuse the pun). Poor management strategies and management practices lay at the heart of the problem. And as with the global financial crisis, it seems that both the regulators and management were unclear about their roles.

Chapter Objectives

- How to develop clear roles within the team

- How to set individual goals that contribute to team success

Chapter theme

The Importance of STRUCTURE and ROLES in developing leadership both individually and as a team.

Who's in charge?

That's the question that was put to the rig's captain, Curt. R. Kuchta by the Coast Guard and Minerals Management investigating committee. On April 20th, before the explosion, there had been a disagreement between a manager from BP (the well's owner) and a manager from Transocean (the rig's owner).

"It's pretty well understood amongst the crew who's in charge", Kuchta answered.

"How do they know that?", asked an investigator.

"I guess I don't know, but it's pretty well . . . everyone knows." He replied.

"Who's in charge?" is indeed the critical question all managers need to ask. In their haste to be more collaborative and effective, many organisations confuse reporting structures with methods of decision making. The two, whilst complimentary, are quite separate.

For example, when an oil rig is first being built and installed, there is a collaborative effort between the well owners, the rig builders and the regulating authority. This is a project working much like a matrix structure in place in many organisations where various stakeholders work together to achieve results.

For start-ups and project teams, matrix structures work extremely well. All involved have clear roles, objectives and tasks. And most importantly, the project is time bound. However, once the project is completed and there is a need for day-to-day management, matrix structures are less successful. "Who's in charge?" is the critical question that must be answered very clearly so that effective decisions are made, the correct people take responsibility for their role, and the manager (or leader) is accountable for results.

But surely committee decisions could be more effective in such circumstances as they engage more people?

Because it takes time - and only because it takes time - committee decision-making in times of crisis, does not work. So, for example when the troops are in the battlefield and the enemy is almost upon them, holding a meeting to decide what to do can only bring one result – disaster!

Thus management needs to be very clear, through well-defined organisation structures, as to "Who is in charge?". It's then a decision for each manager as to the type of decision-making needed for each situation. Such decision-making can range along a continuum from full group consensus to sole decision by the manager with no discussion (you'll recall the following model from the Introduction).

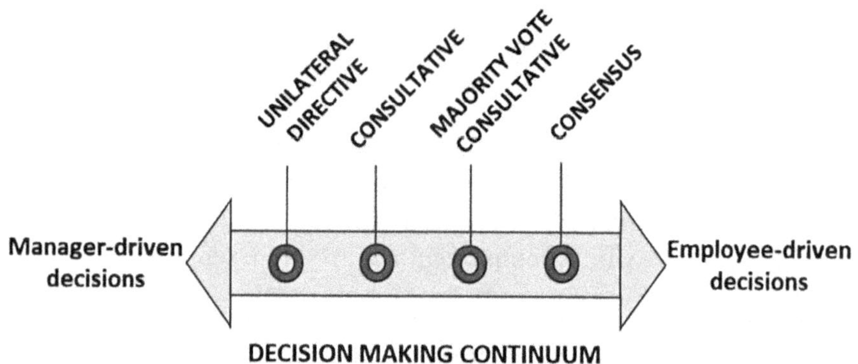

In addition to answering the question "Who's in charge?", we must always be clear on "Who is our customer?". In this case, the Minerals Management Services were unclear as to who their real customer was. Was it the US government or the oil industry?

Apparently, for many years the Minerals Management Services (the US government authority dealing with oil exploration and production) had the dual role of:
- promoting oil exploration in the gulf and
- setting the regulations.

Regulators cannot be marketing to, and regulating, the same people. Compromises (generally resulting in watered down regulations) will always occur to try and attract more business (after all, money does win out!).

Regulators (such as the Minerals Management Services) should always
have only one customer: The Government. And their sole responsibility
must be to ensure the regulations are set and maintained. If the
government then wants to encourage more business, they should set up
a separate entity that is solely responsible for marketing the industry.

At the time, US President Obama, had been looking around for who to
blame for this disaster. And with due cause, he picked on BP. However,
as with other industries such as banking and the airlines, he should also
have looked at how well the various regulating authorities are set up and
managed, and in particular, made sure that they realised what their
exact roles and responsibilities were - most importantly, who their real
customer was – him.

There are two very clear messages for managers to learn from the
Deepwater Horizon disaster:

1. Make sure that the structure enables everyone to clearly answer the
    question "Who's in charge?".

2. Then once that's clear, managers need to be competent and
    confident in applying a range of decision-making processes
    depending on their needs and the situation.

Personal leadership review and learning

1. **What went well or not so well in this event?**
    - Probably nothing went well (at least not when disaster
      struck). So what led to the confusion and finger pointing?

2. **At a personal level, what are the leadership lessons you can
    draw from this story?**
    - How clearly are your team roles defined?

3. **What would I (or my organization, my team) do differently in
    similar circumstances?**
    - Do you need to take any action regarding role clarity? Why/
      Why not?

4. **Is there something I now need to plan for as a result of this learning? If so, what?**

   - In particular, do you believe there is some overlap/under-lap between responsibilities of team members (including your own role)?

Author's note:

In over thirty years of consulting to organisations and managers around the world, one of the most critical elements for success I've noticed, is clear role definition. When looking for the reasons for conflict between a manager and his/her people or between members of the team (or other teams), the first step is to ensure the roles of each person are clear and that no overlap on key tasks or responsibilities occurs (or in some cases under-lap when essential tasks fall through the cracks).

I wrote "Who's in charge?" in June 2010 when all the key players – BP, Transocean and the US government – were at each other's throats as to who was to blame for the hugely damaging oil spill in the Gulf of Mexico. To me it was the classic case of poor role definition. Curt. R. Kuchta (the rig's captain) comments clearly illustrate this point.

The following "Team Learning Exercise" suggests how you could use this (or a similar story of your own) to run a team meeting on the topic of "Role Definition". Now, you may already have perfectly clear and well-defined Job/Role Descriptions in place. My experience suggests that even with the best written Job Descriptions, day-to-day practices can lead to at best role diffusion, and at worst considerable role conflict.

This exercise could also be useful if you happen to work in a matrix structured organisation where role ambiguity can cause confusion and conflict (particularly around reporting relationships).

As Role Definition is such a critical part of team success, you may need to schedule half a day or even a whole day (depending on the size of your team) to complete the following exercise. Alternatively, you may decide to schedule a number of meetings over a longer time period.

Team Learning Exercise

There are lots of thought starters and questions for teams within this story. Here's a suggested way you might use it with your team:

1. Distribute the story of the BP disaster prior to a team meeting and ask everyone to read and answer the following questions (Feel free to pick and choose the questions, or add your own. However, please stick with the discussion on "Outputs" as this is the critical part of role definition):

    - What are the three or four Outputs that I am solely responsible for achieving? ('Outputs' are the results one gets from doing the work, not the tasks undertaken nor the skills used – the latter are 'Inputs' – the two are often confused)
    - What help do I need from other team members to achieve my agreed Outputs?
    - What help could I offer other team members to achieve their Outputs?
    - In addition to being successful in my own role, how will I know when the team is succeeding? What will I see? What will others see? How could these outputs / actions / events be measured?
    - Looking at my own Outputs and the help I have agreed to give to other team members, what would be an objective that I could set for myself that would work toward the team's success?

2. At the meeting ask each team member to list his/her three or four Outputs (make sure each has no more than five) on a flipchart or whiteboard. This should be done at the start of the meeting without discussion (I've found that listing these on flipchart paper and posting the pages around the room is the best way of doing this).

3. Once all people have listed their Outputs, ask the team members to have a good look through all the Outputs of each team member. Without discussion, ask each team member to take a note of those Outputs that are either unclear or overlap with those on someone else's list.

4. Lead a discussion on the Deepwater disaster story each team member has read:
    - What went well or not so well in the Deepwater Horizon Oil Rig disaster?
    - What caused the real problem? Why?
    - What can we as a team learn from that situation?

5. Following the discussion on Deepwater, have each team member in turn read out his/her Outputs:
    - Encourage others to question and clarify as to whether this is an appropriate Output (often they are mistaken as inputs – activities).
    - Is there any overlap with other Outputs from other team members?
    - If there is overlap, reach a decision on where and with whom the Output should reside OR re-word both Outputs so that they are clear, unambiguous and are clearly the responsibility for one team member only.

6. Once all Outputs have been agreed, lead a discussion on "How will we know when the team is seen as being successful?"
    - As a result of this discussion, are there any Outputs people have discerned that are not on anyone's list? If so, agree where they should go.

7. Finally, ask each team member to write a personal objective that will help lead to the team's success (this may be done individually after the meeting and later discussed and agreed with you).

A note on the learning process used here

You may have noticed a three-step process in this suggested team learning exercise:

1. Individual listing of Outputs by each team member (in silence),

2. Group discussion of the BP Deepwater story and its implications,

3. Group discussion of team Outputs and how each member can contribute to team success.

I've found that this three-step process greatly enhances both the richness of the discussion and the resulting actions agreed by team members and the team.

Further suggested reading

Selden, Bob: *"What To Do When You Become The Boss: How new managers become successful managers"* Hachette, 2011 (revised edition 2015).

Birkman: *3 Crucial Steps to Create Role Clarity Within Your Team. Perception Connections; the Birkman blog on perception, personality and organizational success.* https://blog.birkman.com/3-steps-to-create-role-clarity-within-your-team

Points from this exercise to add to my Leadership Plan at the back of the book

STORY 2:
10 SEPTEMBER 2008

Did Plato have the answers to Wall Street's problems?

Almost 2,500 years ago, Plato argued that the endless quest for pleasure affects the kind of leaders that democracies produce. Those who do rise to the top are unlikely to be motivated by concern for the common good, but rather by self- interest. Sound familiar?

Chapter Objectives

- How to help people take personal responsibility

- How to develop distributed leadership within your team

Chapter theme

The Importance of STRUCTURE and ROLES in developing leadership both individually and as a team and how to keep the FOCUS on TEAM, rather than individual.

Did Plato have the answers to Wall Street's problems?

When did you last upgrade your car? (fully electric perhaps?) Your home? Do you have the latest TV, Hi-fi, iPod, iPad or whatever latest techno-whiz available?

Plato (429BC) in The Republic, wrote about the problems of democracy, leading much of the population to seek unnecessary pleasures and the material goods which make these pleasures possible.

He suggested that this endless quest for pleasure affects the kind of leaders that democracies produce – those that have difficulty controlling their desires. Further, he suggested that the most qualified leaders are unlikely to be chosen nor want to serve. And the leaders that do rise to the top, are unlikely to be motivated by concern for the common good, but rather by self-interest. Finally, he posited that this conflict between private and public interest is likely to be endemic.

Is it drawing too long a bow between what Plato was describing and today's society?

Take the case of Lehman Brothers in 2008 where CEO Richard Fuld Jr. kept investing in risky derivatives on the assumption that prices would go up. David Einhorn, hedge fund manager and CEO of Greenlight Capital, on the other hand said back in May that year, that his firm had a short position on Lehman Brothers.

Now here's the interesting bit. Einhorn maintained that he did this not only because Lehman had fudged its numbers, but because its recklessness had put the financial system as we know it at grave risk. Then, at a major financial conference in June of that year, he called on federal regulators to "guide Lehman toward a recapitalization and recognition of its losses - hopefully before federal taxpayer assistance is required" (Lehman Brothers went bankrupt on 15th September 2008).

At the time (June 2008), Einhorn was castigated in certain parts of the press for his comments (this is not the first time he had been so forthright on such issues – see his story on Allied Capital in "Fooling Some Of The People All Of The Time" – Wiley 2010). But he stuck to his position.

Plato would no doubt have been impressed with another insightful quote from Einhorn, "With no one watching, the managements of the investment banks did exactly what they were incentivized to do: maximize employee compensation. Investment banks pay out 50 percent of revenues as compensation. So more leverage means more revenues which means more compensation."

Plato's words might be harsh criticism of today's society (remember he was writing over 2,400 years ago). However, they do have a message for the business, and indeed the wider community. In today's society we need good, no, great leadership, if we are to avoid crises such as the financial meltdown of the GFC.

In this vein, Rob Goffee and Gareth Jones in "Why Should Anyone Be Led by You?" (Goffee and Gareth 2006) talk about the "triumph of individualism" and as a consequence, the need for authentic leadership . . .

"If there is one overriding characteristic of the modern era, it is the extension of personal freedom through the march of individualism. At the heart of this, of course, lies a paradox. While few would deny that modern life has increased the scope for human choice, many have cautioned against the rise of excessive individualism; a world characterized not by the authentic expression of self but as simply selfish." And this was written just two years before the GFC!

So it seems that we need both authentic leaders and systems to curb our excesses. I believe it's a mixture of balancing self (the need for individualism and the maintenance of freedom) with structure (the glue that holds families, communities, organisations and indeed countries, together).

Recent research supports this view. For example, some of the most notable differences between societies revolve around the concepts of 'individualism' and 'collectivism'; whether you consider yourself to be independent and self- contained, or entwined and interconnected with the other people around you, valuing the group over the individual. Generally speaking – although there are exceptions – people in the West tend to be more individualist, and people from Asian countries like India, Japan or China, tend to be more collectivist.

How do we nurture, encourage and develop the necessary 'authentic' leadership - leaders who lean more to a collective rather than individualistic approach? How can we encourage those people that Plato described as "most qualified" to take on leadership roles?

Let's start with the tough stuff – the stuff you and I need to do. But first, here's another question. When was the last time you gave of yourself (not financially, but say, with your time) for the betterment of your colleagues, community, profession or country?

Authentic leadership starts with everyone who is reading this story – we need to set the example by showing leadership ourselves. My suggestion would be to find someone today that you can mentor as a leader for tomorrow. We have all the great leadership training and development initiatives available. But to truly jump-start leadership development, it will mean you and I at a personal and local level, taking the time to mentor the new leaders.

Secondly, we need to re-build structure within organisations and government. Over the last 50 years, organisations have vacillated between centralization and decentralization. That is until the last decade when various forms of matrix organisations have encouraged cooperation across and even between, organisations (although often quite unsuccessfully).

I'm not suggesting a return to the tightly structured organisations of the 1960s and 70s. However, to guide against the inevitable selfishness that is necessary for survival in today's organisation, we need to have underlying structures that hold the organisation together and build cooperative communities.

CEO's have a key role to play here. And at a local level, managers can instigate structures such as cascading performance objectives that link each individual to the team and ultimately, the organisation's mission (not just individual performance goals, but collective performance and cooperation goals).

For better or worse, what gets rewarded, gets done. So let's make collective performance and cooperation goals, "for better".

At a government level, we need to have regulatory authorities that know the difference between their owners and customers, so that they become truly accountable – as I argue in Chapter 21: 'Do You Know Who Your Customers Are?' – this is a critical question for all organisations, departments and teams to settle.

And finally, and perhaps paradoxically, increasing freedom within organisations to make decisions, is exactly what has led to the collapse of some of today's financial icons. We've all preached the virtues (and value) of delegation. However, delegation without maintaining accountability is merely abdication.

When next you and I delegate some key decision making, let's make sure that we maintain accountability for the decisions our people make.

Over the past 100 years, we've now had the great depression, the stock market crash of 1987, the Asian stock market meltdown of 1997, the GFC of 2008 and the economic impact of Covid-19. What's been learnt from these experiences?

Personal leadership review and learning

1. What went well or not so well as a result of the GFC?
    - At first glance, there do not seem to be too many positives that came out of the GFC – are there any? If so, what do they mean for you?

2. At a personal level, what are the leadership lessons you can draw from these and other stories about the GFC?

3. What would I (or my organization, my team) do differently in similar circumstances today?

- No doubt your organisation or industry has made some changes as a result of the GFC, or perhaps of the Covid pandemic. How successful have they been? Why/Why not?

4. Is there something I now need to plan for as a result of this learning? If so, what?

Author's note

You'll notice that I've not suggested any answers to these questions. The intent of this book is to be inquisitive not directive. This process of personal enquiry should lead you to develop your own theory and model of leadership, not be led by others. As in Story 1, there's space for you to record your notes below, or jot them down somewhere where it's easy for you to transfer to your Leadership Plan.

The following 'Team Learning Exercise' suggests how you could use this (or a similar story of your own, e.g. you may wish to make the story more recent, and focus on the economic results of Covid-19 rather than the GFC). to run a team meeting on the topic of 'Taking personal responsibility and leadership within the team'.

Team Learning Exercise

There are lots of thought starters and questions for teams within this story. Here's a suggested way you might use it with your team.

1. Distribute the story (or a copy of this chapter) prior to a team meeting and ask everyone to read and answer the following questions (feel free to pick and choose the questions, or add your own):
   - What can we do as a team that will be of benefit to the community? Are there things we can do as individuals?
   - How do we as a team and as individuals, ensure that bonuses and incentives do not lead us to take unnecessary risks?
   - How do we start a mentoring program, initiative or process to develop some of the younger up and coming people into the leaders of tomorrow?

- What would be some team performance goals that each team member can include in their own performance objectives? i.e. Each team member should have at least one performance objective that directly contributes to the development of the team.
- How do we each delegate responsibility for certain decisions, whilst maintaining our accountability for them? How do we communicate this to others when delegating?

2. At the meeting decide which questions if answered well, will be most beneficial to the team.

3. Lead a discussion on the selected questions to reach consensus on:
   - What action needs to be taken?
   - By whom?
   - By when?
   - How will we measure our results? When?

Further suggested reading

Goffee, R & Jones, G. *Why Should Anyone Be Led by You?* Harvard Business School Press 2006.

Einhorn, D. *Fooling Some of the People All of the Time, A Long Short (and Now Complete) Story,* Updated with New Epilogue. Wiley 2010.

Points from this exercise to add to my Leadership Plan at the back of the book:

SETTING A STRATEGY FOR LEADERSHIP

3. CAN TOO MUCH SUCCESS LEAD TO FAILURE?

- How to improve commitment to team decisions

4. DOES YOUR ORGANISATION PASS THE LONGEVITY TEST?

- How to imbed the organisation's values into day to day behaviour

5. TO OUTSOURCE OR NOT TO OUTSOURCE?

- How to identify your 'real' customers
- How to develop strategies to service your customers

STORY 3:
27 FEBRUARY 2009

Can too much success lead to failure?

A strange phenomenon arose as a result of the recession following the GFC. The most successful companies — those that were used to having the most financial resources and more opportunities - may have been the ones that needed to make the most radical changes in their thinking to weather the storm.

Chapter Objectives

- How to improve commitment to team decisions

Chapter theme

Developing a 'questioning mindset' in all team members when it comes to developing strategy and making strategic decisions.

Can a successful organisation, 'Have its cake and eat it too'?

A colleague in one such successful company at the time of the GFC, told me, "Whenever we get to a decision point where we have to choose between investing in one project or another, in the past we've tended to find a way to choose both by expanding the budget a bit. We have also had the strategy to compete in every market or segment, at every price point, for every sales channel. This means that the typical leadership decision making model has been 'find a way to do it all'. We try to do everything and some of it works, quite a bit doesn't."

The financial situation brought about by the GFC in 2008, suggested that a change was needed in the competencies to run a successful business, particularly in terms of decision-making.

Did these successful companies lack people who had the courage to say "NO" and can see the need for pro-actively making a painful decision? Or more importantly, people who can look at a situation and think differently about how a decision should be made? For example, decisions to kill an activity, pull out from a market up-front in order to secure the remaining activities, or to look at a completely different way of attracting business?

Take the US auto makers who for many years ignored the growing worldwide trend toward smaller, more economic and environmentally friendly vehicles. Using outdated decision making, they were still able to make large profits. Then, despite their financial difficulties following the GFC, their decision making still appeared to be based on false premises.

When sales are down, traditional decision making would suggest "reduce prices". But when customers do not have the money or are unwilling to buy, no price reduction will encourage sales. Dealers in some of the worst affected states even offered a "two for the price of one" deal, which may have brought short term results but perhaps at the expense of long term survival (I've heard of 2-for-1 in many other industries, but not when selling cars!).

Enlightened decision makers on the other hand, instead of looking from their own perspective (of trying to increase sales) might say, "Why are people not buying cars at the moment?" True, some cannot afford to. However, there are many people who have the resources but are unwilling to purchase at the moment. "Why are these people unwilling?"

One car maker took a totally different decision-making approach with stunning results.

In answer to the question "Why are people unwilling to buy at the moment?" they discerned that "people are in fear of losing their jobs, hence they are unprepared to make a commitment to buy a new vehicle irrespective of a price reduction".

So, instead of massive price discounting, they offered a 'returns policy'. The policy covered every buyer of a leased or financed vehicle who involuntarily lost their job, became physically disabled, lost a driver's licence for medical reasons, was transferred to another country, was self-employed and filed for bankruptcy, or died in an accident. They guaranteed to let buyers return their vehicles at no cost and with no loss of their credit rating should they lose their job or income within a year of purchasing the vehicle.

As a result of this type of decision making, Hyundai increased sales in the US by 14% in January 2009 (year on year) and the sales of their Sonata model increased by a staggering 85%! Most other car makers had negative growth, or at best, very modest sales increases – overall, the auto market took a 43% downturn.

Taking a different decision-making approach, Hyundai answered the needs of the buyers' concerns for job security. They increased sales against all the trends.

At the heart of the Hyundai decision making approach, is the oft-quoted, but not so often used, principle of "What's in it for them?"(i.e. the customers). In other words, before looking at one's own needs, identify the needs, interests or concerns of the other party first. And then, "How will satisfying the needs of this stakeholder meet our own needs as well?"

As my colleague whom I mentioned earlier cautioned, "Now we have tougher times and different decisions are needed. It's my feeling that we have to consciously pull out of some markets and focus on the key areas in order to maximise return on more limited investment … but here I see huge challenges for people to make the shift in decision making mindset that would make that possible."

And therein lies the rub – the ability or inclination of people to shift their decision-making mindset.

Perhaps help is at hand. In their book, "Think Again: Why Good Leaders Make Bad Decisions and How to Keep it From Happening to You" (McGraw-Hill 2009), authors Finkelstein, Whitehead, and Campbell, suggest that for many of us the fault lies not so much in our own errors of judgment, but rather in the brain's processes that help create these errors of judgment.

They quote many famous cases (including the US auto makers) of managers and leaders who have made poor decisions. They attribute these to four brain functions:
- the brain's agility in linking the current situation to previous misleading experiences;
- the brain's ability to relate current situations to our pre-judgments of similar situations;
- the brain's inability to separate the situation from personal self-interests; and,
- a tendency to draw an inappropriate emotional link between current stakeholders and those for whom we have strong personal feelings.

The authors suggest some rules to help overcome possible decision-making errors. These are not the typical governance rules. Rather, they are tailored defences against the particular red flags in a given situation (the authors suggest a "red flag" should be raised for each one of these functions in each major leadership decision).

The authors advise leaders to design, for each important decision, a decision process based on an understanding of the red flags that are present at that moment.

So, perhaps the answer for improving the decision-making mindset of leaders and managers is twofold: First, they need to identify the needs, concerns and interests of the other stakeholders; and second, make sure each decision making situation is assessed in terms of the possibility of one or more of the four "red flags".

Would such a mindset overcome my colleague's concerns, when as he says, "Every day I deal with people who have a long list of things that 'we can't even discuss' (when considering cost savings) for various strategic reasons and they believe this almost religiously..."

He continued, "I see a huge danger in this kind of thinking as it prevents some necessary discussions and some difficult decisions from being made when in my opinion this is the time to throw away all these ideas that were formed in a different financial climate and take a totally fresh look at how we want to compete or even survive in the current situation."

Personal leadership review and learning

1. What went well or not so well in this event?
   - The decision-making example in this story is Hyundai's enlightened decision- making versus the outmoded thinking of other US car makers. Which of the four "red flags" do you think Hyundai considered when reaching their decision?

2. At a personal level, what are the leadership lessons you can draw from this and other stories about decision making?

3. What would I (or my organisation, my team) do differently in similar circumstances?
   - It seems as if the other car makers were affected by two or possibly three of Finkelstein's et al four red flags of decision-making. By comparison, why was Hyundai so successful?

4. Is there something I now need to plan for as a result of this learning? If so, what?

Author's note

I wrote this story in February 2009 after an exchange of emails
with a good friend in a major multi-national company. The company
after many years of being the market leader in its segment (they
had a staggering 49% of the market and were so successful that I'm
sure you've probably owned or at least used one of their products),
was rapidly losing ground to new competitors – in fact if the trend
continued, within a few years they might have ceased to exist.

My friend was a dedicated company man and was really concerned
about their decision- making processes. Fortunately, I can report
that after a somewhat lean period, they are now back on track. I can
also report that my friend tells me that the turnaround only came
through some senior managers taking some tough decisions about
reversing the way things had always been done in the past.

Team Learning Exercise

There are some good principles about decision-making inherent
in this story. Teams and leaders make decisions every day – some
of them quite major. Here's a suggested way you might use this
decision-making story with your team.

1. Distribute the story prior to a team meeting and ask everyone
    to read and answer the following questions (feel free to pick and
    choose the questions, or add your own):
    * What is our current method of making decisions?
    * To help discern this, think back to the most recent decision
      we made as a team. What did we do to reach agreement?
    * Who took the lead?
    * Was this leadership effective? Why/Why not?
    * How committed was I to the final decision? Why/Why not?
    * How can we improve the way in which we make decisions?
    * How can I improve my involvement and influence in the team
      decision making process?

2. At the meeting decide which questions if answered well, would
    be most beneficial to the team.

3. Lead a discussion on the selected questions to reach consensus on:
    - What action needs to be taken?
    - By whom?
    - By when?
    - How will our results be measured? When?

Day-to-day Team Decision-making Considerations

For this story, I've added this extra section that you may care to use as a template or checklist when you or your team is faced with making a major decision.

1. Why does this situation differ significantly from previous situations which may at first seem similar?

2. How does the team or organisation stand to benefit personally from a decision in this situation? Is this important in this instance?

3. If another team with different self-interests were making a decision in this situation, what would they do? Should we be guided by this? Why/why not?

4. Do we have strong emotional feelings (either positive or negative) for any stakeholders who might be affected by this decision? If "Yes", what do we need to do to ensure our decision is appropriate?

Further suggested reading

Finkelstein, Whitehead, and Campbell. "Think Again: Why Good Leaders Make Bad Decisions and How to Keep it From Happening to You". McGraw-Hill 2009.

Points to add to my Leadership Plan at the back of the book:

STORY 4:
23 JUNE 2011

Does your organisation pass the longevity test?

Over the last couple of decades, we've seen long-term organisations such as Arthur Anderson, World Com, Enron, Lehman Brothers and many more disappear. In fact, of the top 25 industrial corporations in the United States in 1900, only two remained on that list at the start of the 1960s. And of the top 25 companies on the Fortune 500 in 1961, only six remain there today.

Chapter Objectives

- How to imbed the organisation's values into day-to-day behaviour

Chapter theme

Developing and displaying values at a local team level that will assist the organisation to survive and grow.

Does your organisation pass the longevity test?

Why have so many organisations disappeared? Can we place the blame on the GFC in 2008 (e.g. Lehman Brothers) or lack of corporate governance (e.g. Enron) or perhaps, poor leadership? These may well be the excuses, but they are not the causes.

So, what leads to organisational longevity?

Arie De Geus (who worked for Royal Dutch Shell, founded in 1890) writing in 'The Living Company', suggests that companies are "living entities" that can survive and thrive for centuries if they focus on several aspects of their character and operations.

What are these characteristics?

Well, take IBM as one example – which celebrated 100 years in 2011 – who are on a new wave of success after going through some turbulent times over the previous decade.

Now, in the 1960s the casual observer may have put their success down to IBM's mainframe services. In the 1990s, the same observer may have seen their world dominance of the PC market as the reason for success. In both cases, those observations would be wrong.

What has led to IBM's success over the last century? Is it leadership, charisma, long term thinking?

A Wall Street Journal special supplement (June 16, 2011) celebrating IBM's 100 years, provided some interesting insights about its longevity ...

On Leadership: "We have learned not to confuse charisma with leadership. In business, there are archetypal examples where the genius of a founder created tremendous good fortune - at least in a company's opening act. The cult of personality is seductive".

On Culture: "Watson's (the founder) most enduring contribution to business was his intentional creation of something that would outlast him – a shared corporate culture".

On Values: "Watson showed how the basic beliefs and values of an organization could be perpetuated - to become its guiding constant through time. Values therefore force choices: whom you hire, the ways you serve the customer, how you develop talent at all levels, which businesses you create, enter and exit, and when. Finally, how much risk taking you promote"

On Direction: "We have never defined IBM by what we make, no matter how successful the product or service"

So does IBM's DNA reflect characteristics De Geus referred to? Here's a précis of his four characteristics:

1. Sensitivity to their environment: long-lived companies sample, learn, and adapt to what is going on around them.

2. Persona: they are cohesive and have a strong sense of identity based on the ability to build a shared community.

3. Tolerance: they are patient, generally decentralized, with widespread decision- making authority, and tolerant of "non-core" activities on their periphery (which may well become tomorrow's core).

4. Frugal: they are conservative with their money, which they use to govern their own growth and to provide them with options.

What about some of the iconic companies of today? Will they survive? Do they pass the longevity test? Pick your favourite icon or one that is based in your region (or perhaps your own organisation) and see if it passes the test.

As a proud Australian, at the time of writing this story, I had some concerns for another proud Australian, Qantas. One of Australia's iconic companies, Qantas is the second oldest commercial airline in the world (established in 1920). And like IBM in previous decades, they seemed to be going through some turbulent times in the three or four years following the GFC.

My question was "Will their core values see then through these tough times?"

As Jim Collins and Jerry Porras point out in "Built to Last", "Visionary companies ... had a number of common characteristics; for instance, almost all had some type of core ideology that guided the company in times of upheaval and served as a constant benchmark." Does Qantas have such a core ideology?

Qantas have built their public reputation on safety. Many will remember the famous quote by Dustin Hoffman as the character Raymond in the film Rain Man, who insisted on only flying "Qantas because they have never had a crash". In fact this appears to be an urban myth, as Qantas, particularly pre the jet age, has had a number of crashes over its long history.

As reported in Matthew Benn's book "The Men Who Killed Qantas", whilst safety was a major concern and priority for the founders, in fact the company was built on innovation, service and employee perseverance.

Are these same core values still guiding Qantas? What's happening with them today? What are Qantas' plans for the future? Are they consciously focusing on De Geus' four characteristics for longevity – sensitivity to their environment, persona, tolerance and frugalness?

To help your assessment, here's a snippet of events regarding Qantas that were happening around the period 2010 to 2012:

- They are (or have recently been) in protracted disputes with three sectors of their workforce – pilots, engineers, cabin crew.

- Their safety record has been tarnished with a number of near misses over the last two years.

- Qantas has again slipped down the rankings of the world's best airlines. In the annual Skytrax World Airline Awards of 2011, it was named the world's eighth-best airline, down from number seven in the previous year's awards. The airline has dropped every year since 2008, when it was named the world's third-best carrier.

Finally, Qantas may be losing some support from the Australian public. In a poll conducted by the Sydney Morning Herald (2011) in conjunction with the World Airline Awards' article, of 13,365 people who voted, 45% selected Singapore Airlines (SIA) as their preferred carrier (and SIA do not operate domestically in Australia), while only 12% selected Qantas.

And then there's the competition. The newcomer to the domestic market, Virgin Australia, was rapidly gaining market share. Their target is 30%. To help achieve this, they formed an alliance with Singapore Airlines (No. 2 most popular airline in the world at the time), to provide access for domestic customers to SIA's international frequent flyer program.

So what of the future for Qantas?

CEO Alan Joyce, announced that Qantas would be making some major changes. Key amongst these are a global network of mega alliances and a push into Asia (where salaries and costs are cheaper) to capture growth in premium-priced travel within the region.

I wrote at the time (2011), "It will be interesting to view the results of this strategic change in direction. Will Qantas be celebrating 100 years in 2020? Are they taking heed of what Moid Siddiqui, author of 'Soul Inc.' suggests, '... the real time for a test of values is when a company is not doing well. Downturns must be faced by holding values steadfast, not by compromising them' ".

Have CEO Joyce's major changes worked? Well, there's some good news here ...

Alan Joyce, who joined Qantas as CEO in 2008 has turned the company around through inspirational leadership to such an extent that he had top billing in the Queen's Birthday Honours list of 2017, being appointed a Companion of the Order of Australia (AC) for service to the aviation and tourism industries, gender equity and support of indigenous education.

During his tenure, Joyce has guided the Australian national carrier through a capacity war with Virgin Australia and international airlines; come under fire when he grounded the entire Qantas domestic and international fleet in 2011, saying he did so to "prevent industrial action from killing Qantas"; and copped a lemon meringue pie in the face while he was speaking at a business breakfast in Perth, with the culprit later revealing he was protesting against corporate support for same-sex marriage.

In typical leadership style, Alan Joyce laughed off getting the pie shoved in his face, saying his biggest issue is, "Finding a decent drycleaner. I have been CEO of Qantas now for close to nine years and it was a new experience and I haven't experienced that before. My response is very clearly we live in a democracy. Democracy works when people respect each other's voices, are allowed to talk, be vocal, allowed to say what we believe."

Joyce has given us an example of using positive and affirmative language to start a conversation with key issues for the entire community and clearly setting the tone from the top for longevity at Qantas.

And yes, there was a celebration in 2020! (Note: Skytrax, the leading aviation rating agency, rated Qantas as 4 star post-Covid in July 2021, and they came in at number four in the rankings of the world's best airlines).

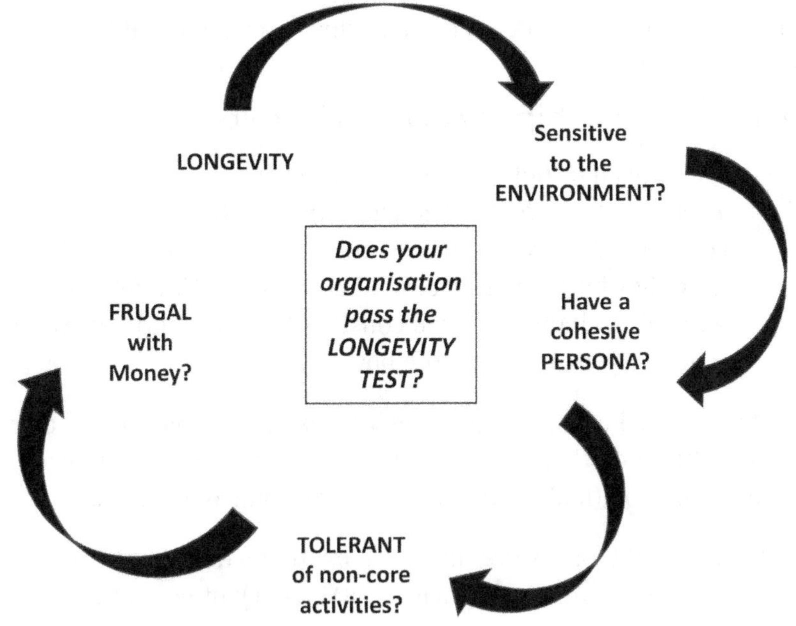

And what of your own organisation? Does it pass the longevity test?

- Is your organization sensitive to its environment? Remember, long-lived companies sample, learn, and adapt to what is going on around them. What changes has your own organisation made over the last ten years as a result of its learning?

- Does your organisation have a persona that is cohesive with a strong sense of identity based on the ability to build a shared community?

- Is your organisation tolerant - tolerant of "non-core" activities on its periphery? Is it patient, generally decentralized, with widespread decision-making authority?

- Is your organisation frugal? Is it conservative with money, which it uses to govern growth and to provide options? (Be careful not to confuse 'frugal' with' cost-cutting' – the former is proactive and looks to provide business growth, whilst the latter is reactive and looks to only control costs).

It's perhaps somewhat easy for us to look at history and analyse why an organisation has succeeded or failed. It's a little more difficult to make future judgments or predictions now – but isn't that the key imperative of the CEO?

Personal leadership review and learning

1. What went well or not so well in this event?
   - There are two events to consider in this story – IBM celebrating 100 years and Qantas at the cross roads. Why have they both been successful up till now? How are they managing change? Do you consider they will both be around in 10 or even 20 years from now?

2. At a personal level, what are the leadership lessons you can draw from this and other stories about companies that seem to keep on keeping on (look at 3M as another example of longevity)?

3. What should I (or my organization, my team) do differently?
   - Underpinning these stories – IBM and Qantas - is the

question of values and how they translate into day-to-day behaviour. Are your team's (or organisation's) values evident in the work that you do and the decisions that you make?

4. Is there something I now need to plan for as a result of this learning? If so, what?

Team Learning Exercise

This story, which involves two iconic organisations – IBM and Qantas – shows how core values can maintain an organisation's existence and what may happen when an organisation drifts away from them. Here's a suggested way you might use it with your team.

1. Distribute the story prior to a team meeting and ask everyone to read and answer the following questions (feel free to pick and choose the questions, or add your own):
   - What are some of the key factors that have led to our organisation's success?
   - Are these factors still in evidence? Of these factors, what's changing or staying the same? Why?
   - Do you think the changes happening in our organisation will affect its long term viability? Why/why not?
   - How would I rate our organisation against De Geus' four characteristics of longevity - sensitivity to their environment, persona, tolerance and frugalness?
   - Of these four, which do we need to do some urgent work on to ensure longevity? Why?

2. At the meeting decide which questions if answered well, would be most beneficial to the team.

3. Lead a discussion on the story and the values your organisation has that will help it survive and grow:
   - What can we as a team do to ensure these values are applied and adhered to on a day-to-day basis?
   - What action needs to be taken?
   - By whom?
   - By when?
   - How will our results be measured? When?

Author's note

If this team exercise proves to be successful, you might consider recommending it to other teams in the organisation and also to communicate the results to your manager or the top team.

It's also interesting to look at the two organisations in this story post-Covid 19. How are they managing the economic fallout of the pandemic? In particular, how is Qantas managing the downturn in both domestic and international travel – are they staying true to their values?

Further suggested reading

De Geus, A. P., *"The Living Company"*, Harvard Business Review Press, 2002. Collins, J.C. & Porras, J.L., *"Built to Last"*, Harper Business, 2004.

Points to add to my Leadership Plan at the back of the book:

WHAT TO DO WHEN LEADERSHIP IS NEEDED

STORY 5:
26 MAY 2011

To outsource or not to outsource?

Since 2009, two of Australia's biggest trade unions have been outsourcing one of their core business activities – member recruitment – to the private sector. The firm, Work Partners employing 90 recruiters, was paid $500 per new union member recruited. As a headline in The Australian newspaper at the time put it, "Unions employ ultimate in outsourcing".

Chapter Objectives

- How to identify your 'real' customers

- How to develop strategies to service your customers

Chapter theme

Structuring an organisation based on identifying your 'real' customers can improve an organisation's efficiency, effectiveness, and ultimately its longevity. Leadership at the top, with a focus on the 'real' customers, can also provide shareholders with a good return on investment.

To outsource or not to outsource?

Since 2009, two of Australia's biggest trade unions have been outsourcing one of their core business activities – member recruitment – to the private sector. The firm, Work Partners employing 90 recruiters, was paid $500 per new union member recruited. As a headline in The Australian newspaper headline put it, "Unions Employ Ultimate in Outsourcing".

Were these trade unions successful in outsourcing?

Brian Henderson, Secretary of the Victorian branch of the Australian Education Union, said at the time that, "The company (Work Partners to whom the work was outsourced) had brought in 7,000 new members from schools, TAFE colleges and early childhood centres over the past two years."

As one would expect, there has been much opposition within union ranks to this scheme. Another union, the Australian Workers Union national secretary, Paul Howes, said that he was opposed to the use of Work Partners. "We don't use them. We are not going to use them as we don't think you can outsource core union work," he said.

Other union officials said the outsourcing recruitment strategy was a "bad look" and a questionable way of addressing declining union membership.

Shift now to May 24, 2011.

The phrase "Ultimate in Outsourcing" in the 2010 The Australian newspaper headline was apparently not 'the ultimate'. You might think that the dissent among union ranks has led to the review of the union's relationship with Work Partners. You'd be wrong – they continued to be employed. Paradoxically, Work Partners has now attempted to outsource its own jobs overseas and devised plans to set up a call centre in The Philippines. So the outsourcing company Work Partners, is now itself outsourcing some of its own activities!

As one would expect, this move by Work Partners has raised concerns. For example, Tony Sheldon, Federal Secretary of the

Transport Workers Union, was reported as saying there had been a "fundamental failure" to have the employees' (the 90 local workers employed by Work Partners) entitlements protected. He also reiterated that there was a danger that contracting out recruitment to a private company would cause a disconnect with workers.

Whilst this may be a local issue and isolated to Australia, it brings into focus the whole notion of outsourcing and offshoring in many, if not most Western countries. What are the benefits to businesses? What are the downsides? In particular, what are the implications for managers who now perhaps have to manage an additional stakeholder – the overseas workforce?

Are benefits such as the drive to gain new members (or customers), cost cutting or financial gain, worth the angst that often comes with outsourcing?

Outsourcing and offshoring have been around for perhaps three to four decades. However, there is still an ongoing debate raging around cost/benefit versus local job loss/retainment. And these are valid issues. They can be particularly relevant to the long term success of the business from both a financial and cultural (organisational) perspective. Outsourcing can impact entire communities and even countries.

The nature of which jobs can be outsourced is also often raised in such debates. For example, many organisations have successfully outsourced some of their back-office jobs - back-office IT outsourcing is quite common. Other functions are also being outsourced. In Australia for example, most local bank branches used to handle all legal (mortgage) documentation. That was then centralised to a department in a capital city (where there was often a high rate of unemployment, and so recruitment was easier). These functions have now been totally outsourced, most notably to firms in India.

But in the headlong rush to outsource everything and reduce overheads (both financial and non-financial), many firms have lost the plot. Now they are outsourcing the sharp end of their business – their customer interface.

Many people reading this will have stories to tell about their experience with an off-shore call centre. Mine came in March 2011.

After more than twenty years with my phone provider, I was threatened with disconnection because I was "approaching my credit limit". The reason? I'd been travelling overseas and global roaming can be expensive. My bills are always paid on time. My current bill was not yet due (in fact I'd not received it). However, the text message on my phone read "if you do not make a payment immediately, your connection will be cut." I made a payment.

I also called the service hot line. Where was this located? Yes, you guessed it, offshore! I became angrier and angrier as the call progressed. The operator had no idea about my long term relationship with the company. Her 'canned' responses to my questions did not satisfy my requests nor appease me.

I immediately looked for another provider. The first question I asked was "Where is your call centre located?" With 'offshore' responses at the first two, I moved on and hit pay-dirt at the third. Not only were they local, but the service I received was far superior to the first two.

As a keen student of management, I decided to find out a little more about the management of my new provider. Is there perhaps something driving this emphasis on service in this organisation?"

To my surprise and delight, I found that David Thodey, CEO of Telstra at the time (my new provider) and his entire senior team had recently spent a day on the phones themselves answering customer service enquiries. The old leadership adage of "Do as I do" was obviously in play here.

Yes, these senior managers needed some training, education and coaching (each had a buddy sitting with him/her whilst on the phone). And yes, as you might expect, they were quite nervous. However, the benefits far outweighed their slight discomfort.

As David Thodey, the CEO said after his experience on the phones, "My respect for our consultants and the way they interact with customers, has always been high. Now it's even higher. . . listening to

 WHAT TO DO WHEN LEADERSHIP IS NEEDED

customers, really understanding what they need, confirming what they say, finding all the information. . . it was great."

David Thodey became Telstra's Chief Executive Officer on 19 May 2009, announcing a strategy of market differentiation and a renewed focus on customer service and satisfaction. He's obviously been true to his word.

One interesting result is the Telstra share price. Until then, the share price had never reached the original float price set 10 years previously. It had been a poor performer. However, since the new CEO came on board, the price steadily increased and at last approached its original float price. Is there a message here for managers and their organisations?

Organisations cannot successfully outsource the sharp-end of their business, whatever that sharp-end may be. It has to be done in-house. How else do you know what your customers want and need? And it's only when managers experience the sharp-end interface that they understand the challenges facing their people. In my own experience as a senior manager in a bank, we were required to spend one week every year working in the branches as Tellers – scary stuff for me, but how beneficial!

There may well be a place for outsourcing certain aspects of the business. However, making that decision requires considerable thought. Will it help achieve the long term goals of the business? Will it support and enhance the corporate culture? How will all the stakeholders (including the community) view the decision?

As the Australian unions discovered, a decision to outsource based purely on cost/benefit analysis, in the longer term is sure to prove costly in more ways than one.

Personal leadership review and learning

1. What went well or not so well in this story? (There are two organisations here, the Australian Workers Union and Telstra)
    *   This story is about identifying just who is your customer?

2. At a personal level, what are the leadership lessons you can draw from this and other stories about the customer interface and customer service? If you do not service external customers directly, when was the last time you interacted with one? What did you learn?

3. What would I (or my organisation, my team) do differently in similar circumstances?
   - Whilst your organisation may or may not outsource any of its functions, the important aspect of this story is to be clear about who your customer is – what are the "sharp end" departments that service the customers' needs? How can you assist?

4. Is there something I now need to plan for as a result of this learning? If so, what?

Author's note:

As a post script to this story, Work Partners went into receivership (the first step towards bankruptcy in Australia) in November 2011 leaving many of its workers without their entitlements (such as long service leave and superannuation).

And there's a further, somewhat disappointing post script to this story. David Thodey who became Telstra's Chief Executive Officer in 2009, (and who had previously had a number of senior roles within IBM), resigned in April 2015.

In early 2016, Telstra commenced outsourcing its customer call centres to the Philippines with the resultant loss of more than 700 jobs locally. A Telstra spokesperson said at the time, "We constantly review the way we work to simplify our business and remove duplication to improve customer experience." Corporate double-talk if ever I've heard it.

By the middle of 2016, Telstra's share price had dropped by 29% and as recently as July 2021 still hovered around the original listing of $2.60 (in 1997). Taking account for inflation, that is a huge drop. And so now, I have a new, local provider.

Team Learning Exercise:

By now you are aware of the intent of this story – to identify who your customers are, then work out the best way of servicing them.

1. Distribute the story prior to a team meeting and ask everyone to read and answer the following questions (you'll need to change some of these questions depending on whether you deal directly with external customers):

    - If you service external customers directly, how would you describe them? i.e. what's their demographic profile?
    - How would you rate the current level of service provided to your customers? Do you have any survey results or direct feedback to support this rating?
    - If you do not service external customers directly, draw a flow diagram representing the supplier/customer flow between your department and the external customer.
    - How would you rate the service you currently provide to the next team/department in your customer/supplier flow diagram? Would they agree with your rating? What tells you that?
    - If you were to suggest some ways that we as a team could improve our service to others, what would these suggestions be?

2. At the meeting decide which questions if answered well, would be most beneficial to the team.

3. Lead a discussion on the selected questions to reach consensus on:

    - What action needs to be taken?
    - By whom?
    - By when?
    - How will our results be measured? When?

Further suggested reading:

Gitomer, J. *"Customer Satisfaction Is Worthless, Customer Loyalty Is Priceless: How to Make Customers Love You, Keep Them Coming Back and Tell Everyone They Know"*. Bard Press, 1998.

Griffin, J. *"Customer Loyalty: How to Earn It, How to Keep It"*, Wiley, 1995.

Points to add to my Leadership Plan at the back of the book:

HOW TO PREPARE FOR THE INEVITABLE *CRISIS* AS A LEADER

6. ARE YOU READY FOR YOUR MURDOCH MOMENT?

- How to prepare for your inevitable crisis

7. WHEN IS AN APOLOGY NOT AN APOLOGY?

- How to get the words 'right' when apologising to various stakeholders

STORY 6:
10 JULY 2011

Are you ready for your Murdoch moment?

As corporate crises go, the one engulfing News International in June/July 2011 was a pretty major one. An organisation is never more vulnerable than when a crisis strikes, but some leaders can handle crises in a way that sets them apart. So what do these leaders do that others do not? And how did News International stack up?

Chapter Objectives

- How to prepare for your inevitable crisis

Chapter theme

Communicating in times of crisis. What to communicate? Who should make statements?

Are you ready for your Murdoch moment?

After 168 years of publication, the British newspaper "News of the World" published its final edition on 10th July 2011. At the time, the newspaper was profitable. News Group Newspapers Ltd., the unit within News International responsible for the News of the World and The Sun, reported an operating profit of 18.2 million pounds in the year ended June 27, 2010.

So what led to the demise of this historic newspaper?

As readers would know from the press stories at the time, the closure was not about profits or profitability (although advertisers were reported as departing rapidly). The closure was about reputation - in particular, the reputation of one of the world's richest men, Rupert Murdoch, CEO of News Corp.

It's been said that leaders emerge in tough times. 'Tough times' can describe natural disasters such as flood, fire, earthquakes or pandemics. These can also be manmade such as war, riots, environmental or economic disasters. And of course companies can experience disasters due to mistakes, malpractice or just plain poor decision making.

In such times, we've seen leaders such as Churchill, Ghandi, Mandala and Jack Welch handle crises in a way that has set them apart as people who were seen as credible and trusted in very trying circumstances.

What is it about these leaders that gives people confidence that despite the pain and hurt it may be causing, the crisis is being well managed? What do these leaders do that others do not?

As Jane Jordan-Meier, author of 'The Four Stages of Highly Effective Crisis Management' says "Nowhere is an organization more vulnerable than when a crisis strikes. Crises are defining moments for organizations and their leaders. They are 'make it or break it moments'."

Where was the leadership at News Corp in the phone hacking scandal as it unfolded in the UK?

Rupert Murdoch had his "make it or break it moment" when he appeared before the UK Parliament Committee hearing.

As Bloomberg's reported, "Rupert Murdoch's refusal to take responsibility for the hacking scandal that has slashed $5.89 billion from the market value of News Corp. (NWSA) may undermine his credibility as Chief Executive Officer."

Governance experts who heard Murdoch's performance before the U.K. Parliament said that by "blaming underlings and saying he wasn't responsible he didn't do enough as CEO to acknowledge his accountability."

Despite describing this as "the most humble day of my life" Murdoch insisted that wrong doing at the newspaper and efforts to clear it up were far below his level.

Is this the behaviour we expect of a leader during a crisis? What should a leader do during a crisis?

When interviewed for this chapter, Jane Jordan-Meier said, "Put simply, the readers and the storytellers themselves, perhaps unknowingly, expect to hear, see and read about stories of courage, death defying events, people surviving against odds, and that someone, somewhere can be held accountable for their losses. There has to be an explanation for why the government took so long to respond, or why there was in-fighting, or why it was yet another tale of bad boys behaving badly. We want to know that someone cares and has the determination, conviction and compassion to do something to make sure that the 'worst' can never happen again. We were hearing very little if anything of this in the phone hacking scandal."

Jordan-Meier's research shows that crises go through four distinct stages:

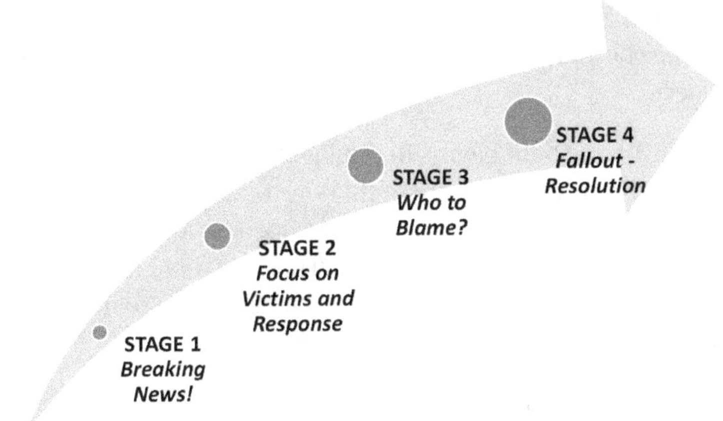

STAGE ONE: the spotlight is beaming squarely on the incident. This is the 'breaking news' stage. "What happened?" is the key question. And the news travels very fast in Stage One to Stage Two – it doesn't take long for the story to jump the 'fire line.'

STAGE TWO: is characterized by the focus on the 'victims' and the response. The light moves quickly from the incident itself (although new facts will continue to emerge) to the 'drama'. How could this have happened? How many people are hurt, missing and/or dead? How is the organisation responding? How quickly did the responders get to the scene? The light will shine brightly on the perpetrator – or who we think the perpetrator might be.

This stage is key. This is the make it or break it stage, the reputation forming stage, the stage where the rallying on social media sites, both negative and positive, becomes a focal point.

STAGE THREE: Stage Three is the one best avoided, although inevitably we all want to go there – yes, the blame, finger pointing stage. Think back to the devastating oil spill in the Gulf of Mexico when the executives of the three companies at the heart of the massive oil spill were severely chastised over attempts to shift the blame to each other.

In this finger pointing stage – everyone has an opinion about you, your product, your organisation, your industry, even your country (ask Malaysia about missing plane MH370) – lots of "woulda, coulda, shoulda."

Stage Three is all about blame with the key question focused on "Why?" The spotlight is more like a floodlight. The crisis is beamed everywhere.

STAGE FOUR: The light begins to dim in Stage Four which is the fallout/resolution stage. The spotlight now dims, but can easily be turned to full glare again if there is a slip up, or something similar happens in the industry. The crisis is perpetually in print, on Google, in Wikipedia – searchable and discoverable. Your "sin" will be for everyone to see forever – you can't take it back.

Typically, this stage marks the end of the crisis; there is some resolution. There might be a funeral, a government inquiry, or a Senate hearing. Your product goes back on the shelf, workers go back to the plant, victims return to their homes.

As Jordan-Meier points out, these stages are very clear "The evidence is plain for all to see. Just watch the media coverage, follow the tweets, notice the Facebook posts and you will soon see the narratives played out in very predictable patterns, with very predictable questions." That's the good news.

And the bad?

Well, it happens at lightning speed, so be prepared to make a statement within an hour of something happening.

Jordan-Meier also points out there is a need for a recognised and credible spokesperson to handle each stage, "Communicating in a crisis is not for the faint-hearted or the un-trained. In a crisis, you need speed, decisiveness, authority and often significant courage. Jack Welch says that even those who are 'extraordinarily gifted' try to make the problem 'disappear' by giving it to someone else to solve. Indeed, not the best strategy. The choice of spokesperson is a critical component for effective crisis management. Crises have the potential to destroy entire industries, bring down governments, and adversely affect large regions of the globe."

How did Murdoch handle these stages?

    WHAT TO DO WHEN LEADERSHIP IS NEEDED

When the story started to break in early July 2011, News Corp. hired two public relations advisers to assist the company during its phone hacking scandal – "Sard Verbinnen & Co. in New York and Glover Park Group in Washington will work with the company's communications, investor relations and government teams", Julie Henderson, a News Corp. spokeswoman, said in an interview by Bloomberg. This is the 'breaking news', the 'what happened?' stage. Julie Henderson is Senior Vice President, Communications and Corporate Strategy, and despite the impressive title, sits below the senior management team level.

Was this an appropriate response to Stage One – the 'breaking news' stage? Was Julie Henderson the appropriate spokesperson? And what of the delegation to PR firms?

Then the phone hacking story quickly moved to Stage Two. As Jordan-Meier points out,

"Stage Two is where the focus shifts to the victims and the response from the government or organisation". In this case, the incident that really triggered the huge public outcry in the UK was the phone hacking of murdered school girl Milly Dowler.

The News Corp response? The first was to close the newspaper, News of the World. Would this make the crisis go away?

Then, in short succession there were resignations from key News Corp executives. Notable amongst these was Rebekah Brooks, CEO of News International, the company responsible for the UK operations. The scandal had now also caused the resignation of two of the UK's top police.

Where was the key crisis management spokesperson in Stage Two?

Finally, Murdoch appears and provides a personal apology to the family of Milly Dowler.

Remember, Stage Two is key. This is the make it or break it stage, the reputation forming stage, the stage where the rallying on social media sites, both negative and positive, becomes a focal point - How did Murdoch score? Apparently, Murdoch made a personal apology to Milly Dowler's parents. However, there was no public apology and it was left to Murdoch's lawyers to report to the public on his personal apology.

We've now moved very clearly into Stage Three – the 'blame', 'finger pointing' stage. Rupert Murdoch and his son James, now CEO of BSkyB, the UK television arm of News International, appeared before a UK parliament investigating committee. Whilst it appears that James' reputation may have been enhanced, Rupert fared less well.

"The News of the World is less than 1 per cent of our company," Murdoch told Parliament's Culture, Media and Sport Committee. He said he may have "lost sight" of the paper because it was "so small in the general frame of the company." Is this an appropriate response to capably manage Stage Three?

Stage Four probably started with the punch thrown by Rupert's wife in the parliamentary enquiry. The Murdochs' appearance before MPs for a grilling about the phone-hacking scandal was brought to a dramatic halt after an activist attempted to hit Rupert Murdoch in the face with a paper plate covered in shaving foam.

Murdoch's wife Wendi Deng, who was sitting behind her husband at the Culture, Media and Sport Committee hearing, leapt up to defend her husband and appeared to hit out at the attacker as security guards and police rushed across the room to apprehend him. (Stage Four includes fallout).

From a leadership perspective, the important thing for all of us to consider is "Could this happen to me?" We may think we are immune to crises, yet who can predict the future? Remember, crises can occur for any number of reasons – some of which are outside our control.

The one thing we can do however is be prepared. Does your organisation have a crisis management plan in place? Are there designated spokespeople to handle each of the stages? Has everyone been trained? Are you ready to handle your crisis?

 WHAT TO DO WHEN LEADERSHIP IS NEEDED

Personal leadership review and learning

1. What went well or not so well in this story?
   - This story is about governance and crisis management.

2. At a personal level, what are the leadership lessons you can draw from this and other stories that report crises? Has your organisation experienced a crisis similar to this? Where are the potential 'fault lines' in your organisation, or perhaps your team?

3. What would I (or my organisation, my team) do differently in similar circumstances?
   - The key considerations here, are, "Does my organisation have a crisis management plan? How well known and understood is it?"

4. Is there something I now need to plan for as a result of this learning? If so, what?

Author's note:

In June 2014, the press reported; "Former News of the World editor and Downing Street spin doctor Andy Coulson has been found guilty of phone hacking, but Rebekah Brooks has been cleared on all counts and has walked free from the Old Bailey's marathon phone hacking trial. The verdict prompted British Prime Minister David Cameron to issue a 'full and frank' apology for hiring Coulson as his communications director, despite having received private warnings about the phone hacking claims."

Team Learning Exercise:

By now you are aware of the intent of this story – to identify who your customers are, then work out the best way of servicing them. And more particularly, how to manage the relationship in a crisis.

1. Distribute the story prior to a team meeting and ask everyone to read and answer the following questions (you'll need to change some of these questions depending on whether you already have a crisis management plan in place):

- What governance policies and procedures does your organisation have in place? Are people familiar with what's required in their role in regard to ethics?
- How would you rate the current level of openness in your organisation? Can people report wrong doing or potential wrong doing by a colleague to their manager without fear of being criticized or indeed castigated?
- What's the procedure for handling a crisis in your organisation? Who are the designated spokespeople? Have they been trained?

2. At the meeting decide which questions if answered well, would be most beneficial to the team.

3. Lead a discussion on the selected questions to reach consensus on:
   - What action needs to be taken?
   - By whom?
   - By when?
   - How will our results be measured? When?

Further suggested reading:

Jordan-Meier, J., *"The Four Stages of Highly Effective Crisis Management"*, Boca Raton, FL : CRS Press, 2011.

Points to add to my Leadership Plan at the back of the book:

STORY 7:
15 JANUARY 2019

When is an apology not an apology?

When organisations get caught in a crisis either of their own making or otherwise, there is often an apology that has to be made to various stakeholders. Why do some of these messages sound credible and display empathy, whilst others smack of insincerity?

Chapter Objectives

- How to get the words 'right' when apologising to various stakeholders

Chapter theme

Communicating in times of crisis, particularly when the organisation has made a major error or been caught in a scandal of some sort.

When is an apology not an apology?

In December 2018, New Zealanders experienced a collective feeling of shame. It was Sunday 9th December and UK tourist Grace Millane's body had just been found in bushland in western Auckland.

Prime Minister Jacinda Ardern, visibly emotional, issued the following statement: "There is this overwhelming sense of hurt and shame that this has happened in our country, a place that prides itself on our hospitality, on our manaakitanga," she said, using the Māori word for welcoming others.

"So on behalf of New Zealand, I want to apologise to Grace's family – your daughter should have been safe here and she wasn't, and I'm sorry for that."

With that statement, whilst still feeling sad for this horrific event, all New Zealanders moved from a feeling of 'shame' to one of 'pride' – pride in our ability to show that we could emphasise with the hurt of the Millane family.

Compare the impact of this statement with that issued by Quinovic, the Wellington (NZ) based property management company that got into strife over its advertisements that were branded as 'racist', when their ads to property owners declared, "Cheers to you! Are you financing your tenant's social life?" - superimposed over a number of half-empty beer and wine glasses.

Their statement of apology read:

"Quinovic Te Aro would like to wholeheartedly apologise for the recently released campaign. The message was not at all intended to be offensive to tenants. Quinovic Te Aro highly values its tenants and once again we offer our sincere apologies for any offence this may have caused."

Why did Jacinda Adern's apology get reported worldwide with overwhelming admiration, whilst Quinovic's was not seen as sincere by many tenants and was taken down from Quinovic's Facebook page the following day?

   WHAT TO DO WHEN **LEADERSHIP IS NEEDED**

Was it the emotional state evident in Ardern's delivery? Was it the words she used? Why did one apology move us from one emotional state to another, whilst the other kept the intended audience in one of anger?

It is both the delivery and the words – and surprisingly, using the right words can impact the delivery.

The words 'apologise' and 'sorry' have two different impacts on both the speaker and the audience. 'Apology' is a noun, "I wish to make an apology". It can be analysed, dissected, debated, argued over – and it goes straight to the reasoning part of the brain. 'Sorry', on the other hand, is an adjective – it describes a feeling of sadness "I'm sorry I hurt you". It can't be described, analysed or dissected – and it goes straight to the feeling part of the brain.

The word...	What is it?	Descriptions...	Impact? It cannot be:	Goes to...
'Apologise'	Noun	"I wish to make an apology" "We apologise unconditionally" "We sincerely apologise"	✓ analysed, ✓ dissected, ✓ debated, ✓ argued over.	REASONING part of the brain

Apologies using the word "apology" are often seen and taken as insincere.

The word...	What is it?	Descriptions...	Impact? It can be:	Goes to...
'Sorry'	Adjective	"I'm sorry I hurt you" "We're sorry that this caused upset" "We're sorry for our mistake. We will correct it"	× analysed, × dissected, × debated, × argued over.	FEELING part of the brain

Apologies using the word "sorry" are mostly seen and taken as sincere.

Apart from not saying 'sorry' for hurting others, there are also further issues with a formal apology such as that issued by Quinovic. Most formal apologies, whilst rarely using the word 'sorry' also make the mistake of using what psychologists call 'qualifiers' words such as 'wholeheartedly', 'sincere', 'honestly', 'to be honest', or 'unconditionally' and people see through these immediately and label the entire apology as insincere.

The other main difference between these apologies, is that one was personal – given by Ardern on behalf of the New Zealand people – she personalised it using the words 'New Zealand', 'Grace's family' and 'I'm sorry'.

Companies, government departments, anyone who has hurt anyone else, needs to:

- ensure that their apology is sincere,
- given from their personal perspective,
- and contains the word 'sorry'.

And it should contain no reason as to why the mistake or event occurred – that may be for another time, and another place. People just want to hear and feel that the speaker is genuinely sorry for causing the hurt.

There's a spurious argument that saying "sorry" may imply
negligence or imply financial retribution. It does not. For example,
it's been reported that in the US, for too long doctors, nurses, and
other clinicians have been told never to say the word "sorry", lest
they buy the hospital, practice, or insurance company a lawsuit. Yet,
it's now known that the absence of 'sorry' is one of the chief drivers
of medical malpractice litigation in the US. Seasoned litigators say
patients and families often mention it during depositions: "Nobody
ever said sorry."

A study published in the Journal of Patient Safety and Risk
Management found that hospital staff and doctors willing to
discuss, apologize for, and resolve adverse medical events through
a "collaborative communication resolution program", experienced
a significant decrease in the filing of legal claims, defence costs,
liability costs and time required to close cases. For instance, the
study found that for events that contained medical errors, these
events were resolved by 'apology' alone in 43% of the cases.

And for those wishing to get some guidelines on how to say "sorry"
and mean it, the New Zealand Privacy Commissioner's website has an
excellent article "How to say sorry". As their article suggests, "Very
often, we find that complainants who have a sense of hurt and anger
due to the actions of an agency, simply want that hurt recognised,
and for an apology to be issued. In many situations, apologising is
simply the right thing to do, and agencies recognise that."

Personal leadership review and learning

1. What went well or not so well in these stories of Ardern and
    Quinovic?
    - Which words worked, and which didn't?

2. At a personal level, what are the leadership lessons you can
    draw from this and other stories that report apologies? Has your
    organisation had to apologise publicly? How well did it go? What
    was the outcome? What other public apologies have you seen or
    heard lately that felt insincere?

3. What would I (or my organisation, my team) do differently in similar circumstances (e.g. the Quinovic case)?
    • The key consideration here is, "Have the key people in my organisation been trained in how to make a genuine apology?"

4. Is there something I now need to plan for as a result of this learning? If so, what?

Author's note:

You'll note that the emphasis in these stories has been the use of the word 'sorry' to express empathy – and expressing empathy is the key, otherwise it is not meaningful.

Unfortunately, we've been trained since childhood to use the word 'sorry', when apologising for small indiscretions such as "I'm sorry I interrupted you", "I'm sorry I'm late", or "I'm sorry for my poor handwriting" – none of these has really hurt the feelings of the other person – it's just a simple mistake – and so 'sorry' may seem to have lost its true impact.

However, when used in important crises or 'stuff up' communications, and in a show of respect for others and the impact on their feelings that your action has had, it can be the most powerful word in the English language!

Team Learning Exercise:

The intent of this story is to learn how to make a genuine apology in times of crisis.

1. Distribute the story prior to a team meeting and ask everyone to read and answer the following questions:
    • What major mistakes have been made by the organisation (or the team)?
    • Who was impacted by these mistakes or errors?
    • How was the apology handled? What words were used? Would they have impacted the aggrieved party appropriately?
    • What were the results or outcomes of the apology (not the error)?

2. Lead a discussion on the questions to reach consensus on:
    - What action needs to be taken if future stuff-ups occur and an apology needs to be given?
    - By whom should it be given?
    - By when?
    - How will our results be measured? When?

Further suggested reading:

Ackerman, B. *You Had Me at "I'm Sorry": The Impact of Physicians' Apologies on Medical Malpractice Litigation,* Healthcare Medical Malpractice, November 6, 2018.

Cahill, L. *How To Say Sorry,* NZ Privacy Commissioner, 13 February 2017.

Points to add to my Leadership Plan at the back of the book:

DEVELOPING PERSONAL LEADERSHIP

8. TOUGH TIMES CALL FOR TOUGH LEADERSHIP

- How to develop an enquiring culture within your team
- How to develop a positive language for listening to new ideas and suggestions for change

9. WHY ISN'T GOOD LEADERSHIP RECOGNISED?

- How to encourage leadership within the team

10. WHERE HAVE ALL THE HONEST MANAGERS GONE?

- How to develop the 'ideal team'

STORY 8:
12 DECEMBER 2008

Tough times call for tough leadership

What do business leaders do when confronted by a downturn? As in previous recessions, their responses tend to fall into four main areas.

Chapter Objectives

- To commence the development of an enquiring culture within your team – i.e. to regularly question the status quo without fear of reprisal.

- To develop a positive language for listening to new ideas and suggestions for change.

Chapter theme

Inclusive leadership – encouraging team members to be creative, innovative and suggest different ways of doing things – without fear of recrimination.

Tough times call for tough leadership

What do business leaders do when confronted by a downturn? The following examples are taken from organisations experiencing the 'financial crush' of the GFC in 2008. Their responses tend to fall into four main areas:

- They can reduce operational costs and defer capital expenditure. That's the approach adopted by mining giant, Rio Tinto, which cut operating costs by $2.5 billion per year and more than halved its capital expenditure to $4 billion.
- They can review operating procedures, tighten controls and upwardly delegate decision-making approvals so that expenditure is tightly controlled.
- They can narrow the business scope or reduce prices on products and services in the hope that people will buy more.
- Or they can cut staff numbers, something that companies such as Sony began to do when it announced plans to cut 8,000 jobs and shut one in 10 of its electronics manufacturing sites.

Looking at these leadership strategies, it is striking that they are all-top down decisions. There seems to be a thinking among business leaders that leadership is best displayed by taking the approach of "call the shots", "carry the ball", "make decisions!".

Do these types of strategies work?

Well, the stock markets seem to think so, particularly in the short term. It's quite noticeable that shares in companies that take these measures invariably rise. For example, Rio Tinto's shares rose 10 per cent when its new measures were announced.

But what happens in the long term?

PriceWaterhouseCoopers reported that following the 2002 downturn, nearly 60 per cent of global CFOs conceded that the costs they were then currently cutting, would creep back into the business within two to three years.

And that's just the cost creep. What happens when the economy starts moving again – are these organisations flexible enough to re-hire, re-train and re-develop lost markets?

What's needed in times like this are not the sort of short-term, top-down balance sheet approaches we see being taken. Rather a style of leadership that is inclusive and cooperative but still tough, might be the best way to go.

In a Harvard Business Review article, 'Leading from the Base of the Beanstalk', Tamara J. Erickson argues that leaders need to take a quite different approach:

- Ask great questions – "Challenge the organisation to respond (to the current situation) by setting intriguing and complex goals. Articulate a compelling mission that will get people to rally".
- Build trust across the organisation – "Don't cut out meetings, or intensify internal competition, or reduce investments in learning. Increase your firm's collaborative capacity by building relationships and encouraging the exchange of knowledge"
- Challenge the status quo – "Ensure that your team is regularly exposed to diverse points of view and experiences"

How might such leadership strategies work in practice?

The simple answer is to ask the people. What might happen for instance, if the company leadership said, "We need to reduce costs by 20 per cent - what are your suggestions for doing that?"

They just might find that employees come up with some stunning suggestions. Suppose that staff said, "We can reduce costs 20 per cent by taking a reduction in pay - working four days a week instead of five".

Unbelievable, you might say? Well, staff and management at Corus, the huge UK steel maker (owned by Tata of India) suggested a 15 per cent cut in pay as a sop against job losses. Yes, not senior management, but everyone below that level made the suggestion!

Now, take Sony's 8,000 electronics job cuts – the equivalent of five per cent of its workforce. How much more would they have saved if the 160,000 employees decided to take a 10 per cent, 15 per cent or even 20 per cent pay cut? And think of the 8,000 jobs this would save.

Would staff be motivated to suggest such initiatives? Well, in today's uncertain times, which would you prefer, a cut in pay or a loss of job? In stressful economic times, job security is a key motivator.

The question is, are leaders tough enough to take the risk to involve their people?

Personal leadership review and learning

1. What went well or not so well in these short examples?
    - This story is about "inclusive leadership". How do I rate myself as a leader who involves people to get the best results? How do I handle it when one of my team suggests something that I think is "way out of bounds"? What do I say in response?

2. At a personal level, what are the leadership lessons I can draw from this and other stories about leadership decision-making in tough economic times? Would I be bold enough to suggest some of the approaches Tamara J. Erickson recommends?

3. What would I (or my organisation, my team) do differently in similar circumstances?
    - You may currently be in similar, challenging circumstances. What are you and your team doing to meet these challenges?
    - Is there something I now need to plan for as a result of this learning? If so, what?

Author's note

This story and the subsequent meetings you may have with your team are all about developing a culture where people are prepared to speak up when they disagree with a decision. Be sure you are ready to take this step before using the following exercise, as once started, the culture will continue to develop unless your actions tell the team otherwise. For example, you may run this meeting; get everyone excited, then when someone comes up with something that you disagree with, 'jump on them'. To be inclusive, you need to look at situations through another lens – a lens that might be quite different to your present eye-wear.

Further note: You may care to focus these discussions on how your organisation handled the Covid-19 economic downturn, or bring up some other examples of organisations that approached the Covid challenges in a different way (or even perhaps the differences between how various countries managed the challenge of the pandemic).

Team Learning Exercise

There could be a lot of ground to cover on this topic of decision making and 'inclusion' in your team. You may therefore wish to split the following team exercise into two, or possibly three sessions.

There are some good principles about decision making inherent in this story. Teams and leaders make decisions every day – some of them quite major. Here's a suggested way you might use this decision-making story with your team.

1. Distribute the story prior to a team meeting and ask everyone to read and answer the following questions (feel free to pick and choose the questions or add your own and please stick to the general principles and basic script).

   Ask people to write out their answers to the following questions before they come to the meeting – it's important for this meeting to be successful, that everyone has had some individual thoughts before they discuss it with others (the following questions are their pre-work for the meeting):

   1. What's changed in the way we go about things over the last (insert here the timeline you intend to discuss, say two years, or the time since the last major challenge your organisation faced, or perhaps since Covid hit)?
   2. Are these changes working for us? What else can we do? Why?
   3. If you were asked to reduce costs by say 20%, what would you do? Where would you start? Why?
   4. How would you suggest we gain more staff involvement in decisions we make?

2. Run a discussion around the four pre-work questions. During the discussion, make sure to stick with the ground-rules listed below.

N.B. These questions, particularly the last one on 'staff involvement' are likely to garner some feedback (perhaps a little obtusely) about your own leadership style. Make sure you are prepared to take this step before including this question in the discussion.

1. Take each question in turn (You'll need to divide the meeting time into four sections, one for each question – allow more time for those that are likely to produce the most discussion).
2. Each person takes it in turn to read out his/her answers without discussion.
3. Other team members are only permitted to say:
    - Tell me more...
    - For instance?
    - Can you give me an example please?
    - Can you clarify that a little further please?
    - No discussion of the idea is permitted at this stage.
4. List all this person's ideas on a whiteboard/flipchart or similar as they are read out.
5. Next team member then reads out his/her ideas – same rules for listening apply.
6. When all team member ideas have been listed, lead a discussion to reach consensus on the ideas that are most pertinent or likely to work.

3. Once consensus has been reached on the best ideas, reach agreement on:
    - What action needs to be taken to ensure these ideas will be implemented?

- By whom?
- By when?
- How will our results be measured? When?

4. Once your Action Plan has been completed, conclude the discussion on the ideas to reduce costs. The meeting now moves to discuss decision making and putting forward ideas that challenge the status quo. Your discussion-leading questions should run along the following lines:
   - What led to such a good discussion on this topic? Why? (Answers may include; pre-work, time to think before the meeting, ability to speak up without being criticized, opportunity to put my ideas across without interruption, able to ask clarifying questions, and so on).
   - How can we (as a team) ensure we have more productive meetings similar to this one?
   - What can each of us do personally to ensure people are free to suggest different ways of doing things?
   - What would you suggest I do as your manager to continue to encourage this culture of inclusiveness and questioning?

N.B. Make sure the discussion does not move back into talking about the ideas the team has already agreed on re costs. This part of the meeting is now about process – how we make decisions and leadership – not about content (e.g. costs).

Further suggested reading:

Erickson T., *Leading from the Base of the Beanstalk*, Harvard Business Review, 21 May 2010.

Points to add to my Leadership Plan at the back of the book:

STORY 9: 31 JULY 2009

Why isn't good leadership recognised?

"He lets others take the limelight. He encourages his people to make decisions. He delegates. He asks for others' opinions before giving his own". Sounds like great leadership to me. So why were so many people sniping at James L. Jones, President Obama's national security advisor?

Chapter Objectives

- To identify leadership behaviours displayed in our organisation

- To foster a culture within our team that will help team members develop some of these leadership behaviours

Chapter theme

Is leadership style – as seen by others – as important as the results a leader achieves?

Why isn't good leadership recognised?

In July 2009, there was a story about an interesting US executive. "He goes cycling at lunch time, leaves work early (apparently 7.30 pm is considered early at his level) and takes a 'bottom up' approach to leadership. Who is he? James L. Jones, President Obama's national security advisor."

When asked by reporters about other White House officials who work deep into the night, he responded "Congratulations. To me that means you're not organized".

I can relate to the sniping by other White House staff about Jones' work hours. As a newly appointed senior manager in a large regional bank some years back, I used to leave no later than 6.pm. I heard from trusted colleagues that people were saying that , "Bob's not working hard enough", or "He doesn't seem to be pulling his weight". However, I started work at 7am whereas others started around 9am or even later.

The bank had a culture of working late into the night. In fact, there's a story (true) about a young man who was regularly seen by the CEO as one of the last to leave – this man was made PA to the CEO and eventually became CEO! It seems that sometimes, it's not what you achieve that's important, but how you're seen.

In his time as National Security Advisor, Jones displayed a different style of leadership, as he described it a "bottom up" approach – he takes a back seat, letting others take the limelight; encourages his people to make decisions; delegates to key aides; regularly asks for others' opinions before giving his own. He's even sent staff members to the Oval Office on his behalf for meetings with the President.

As Jones commented, "You can be a leader that takes charge of every meeting and takes charge of every issue and rides it to conclusion and play a very dominant role. For me that has the effect of muting voices."

What a refreshing change from many of the so called leaders we often see in politics, administration and even corporate life. Surely

Jones' behaviour epitomizes the description of real leadership so often given by our leadership gurus?

But, and there has to be a "but", as I wrote this story in 2009, I pondered, is Jones going to last the distance? Perhaps in the culture within which he is working, the 'top down' leadership style of being decisive (even though the decision may turn out to be wrong) is greatly valued. People expect their leaders to be seen. They expect them to make strong statements. They may even expect them to work late into the night!

After all, isn't that the style that got Bush elected for his second term? He was "seen" to be doing things.

I wondered, "Will Jones' peers, his boss, the press (apparently he shuns the press and has had only one press conference since taking office) and the general public see the virtue of his style? Or will the sniping continue until it becomes back stabbing and fatal?"

A story at the time in the New York Times, (Friday May 6, 2009) 'National Security Advisor Tries Quieter Approach', regarding his management style, raised an interesting question. Why was there any need for an article on his management style? Whilst the piece was quite balanced in its reporting, why report extensively on his style rather than the results he was achieving? This does seem a leadership culture issue (as a side issue, it's interesting to note that some social psychologists have posited that the media actually reflect the culture of the nation – interesting . . .).

Was he achieving results? It seems so. For example, his 'behind the scenes processes' apparently set up the very favourable NATO deal for Obama with Turkey and he was instrumental in improved South American - US relationships.

I find it interesting that Jones came out of the army. He was a four-star general and supreme commander of NATO. Perhaps the army has a somewhat different culture where results and not image, matter? Decisions in the army affect life – and death.

Jones lasted until October 2010, when he was replaced by a more conventional (and probably politically wilier) manager, Thomas E. Donilon.

Leaders must be trusted and followed for their ability to achieve results. In the political arena into which Jones had been thrust, it seems that unfortunately image is perhaps more important.

Why isn't good leadership recognized for what it is? – good leadership!

Personal leadership review and learning

2. What went well or not so well in this story?
    - On the surface, this appears to be about good leadership, and perhaps it is. As the story heading posits; "Why isn't good leadership recognised?

3. At a personal level, what are the leadership lessons you can draw from this? Have you seen people within your organisation that you have deemed to be very successful leader/managers, only to see them be undone by the culture? What does this mean for your own leadership style?

4. What would I do differently in similar circumstances?

5. Is there something I now need to plan for as a result of this learning? If so, what?

Author's note

James L. Jones resigned from his post as National Security Advisor in October 2010. As the Washington Post reported at the time ". . .Jones, a towering if aloof figure, often had trouble fitting into a National Security Council culture dominated by several hard-charging veterans of Obama's campaign who have known the president for years. His condition for initially taking the job - that he would be the last one to see Obama on the most pressing national security issues of the day - was often unmet.

"I think in many ways he was underrated," said a White House official, who like others spoke on the condition of anonymity to discuss internal personnel assessments, "But there has been a lame-duck quality to this for months".

Jones made clear that he intended to serve no more than two years. But several administration officials said that his departure was accelerated by the publication of Bob Woodward's book 'Obama's Wars,' which portrayed Jones as a deeply unhappy figure often on the edge of important policy decisions.

After leaving the Obama administration, Jones returned as a Fellow at the US Chamber of Commerce in 2011.

The board of directors of General Dynamics elected Jones as a director of their corporation in 2011. Also, in 2012, Jones joined Deloitte Consulting LLP as a senior adviser to work with Federal and commercial consulting clients within Deloitte's Department of Defense and Intel segments. In early 2013, Jones joined OxiCool Inc's Advisory Board.

In his retirement, Jones is now a Trustee of the US Center for Strategic and International Studies.

Team Learning Exercise

There appears to be an important message about leadership style in this article. Here's a suggested way you might use this leadership story with your team.

1. Distribute the story prior to a team meeting and ask everyone to read and answer the following questions before attending the meeting (feel free to pick and choose the questions, or add your own and please stick to the general principles and basic script).
    - Think of the most successful managers in our organisation. What are the things they do that make them so successful? List as may behaviours as you can think of that you've noticed they display.
    - Now pick out the two or three really outstanding managers (no need to use names, but do keep these particular people in mind as you answer this question). What are the two or three things these managers do that really set them apart from all of the rest?

2. Open the meeting with a general discussion about this article
    and what "leadership style" means. Then, run a discussion
    around the following two pre-work questions:
    - What are the behaviours people identified that are displayed
      by the good managers in the organisation? (these could be
      described as the "management competencies" required to be
      an effective manager in our organisation).
    - What are the small number of behaviours that are displayed
      by the exceptional managers? These are most likely to be
      the behaviours that set leaders apart from managers in our
      organisation.
    - Further general discussion questions:
      » Are the "exceptional managers" (leaders) recognised as
        such by the hierarchy? Why/Why not?
      » What does this mean for career development?
      » What can we do within our team to start reinforcing
        some of the behaviours (in each other) that we've
        identified that set leaders apart?

Further suggested reading:

Covey, S.M.R., *How the Best Leaders Build Trust,* Leadership Now,
https://www.leadershipnow.com/CoveyOnTrust.html

Points to add to my Leadership Plan at the back of the book:

STORY 10: JUNE 2008

Where have all the honest managers gone?

It emerged last week (June 2008) in Germany that Deutsche Telekom spied on thousands of its own employee's (and director's) phone messages in an attempt to identify the source of leaks to the media.

Chapter Objectives

- How to develop the 'Ideal Team'

Chapter theme

Honesty at work. How managers can engender a culture of positivity and honesty within the team.

Where have all the honest managers gone?

It emerged last week (June 2008) in Germany that Deutsche Telekom spied on thousands of its own employee's (and director's) phone messages in an attempt to identify the source of leaks to the media.

Is the Deutsche Telekom incident another example (think also Hewlett-Packard spying on board members, Samsung cheating on its energy ratings) where trust within an organisation has broken down? Are these isolated instances, or is there a deeper, ingrained 'honesty' problem within some organisations that may eventually lead to mistrust?

Where have all the honest managers gone? According to one study, they seem to be disappearing at quite a rate.

The Leadership Quarterly reports that a 2008 study found many bosses are seen as dishonest. The study specifically pointed out the widespread perceptions that underpin this belief:

- 39 per cent of those surveyed said their supervisors had failed to keep promises.
- 37 per cent said their supervisors had failed to give credit when due.
- 31 per cent said their supervisors had given them the "silent treatment" in the past year.
- 27 per cent said their supervisors had made negative comments about them to other employees or managers.
- 24 per cent said their supervisors had invaded their privacy.
- 23 per cent said their supervisors had blamed others to cover up mistakes or to minimise embarrassment.

Florida State University, the authors of the report, suggest that such dishonesty not only affects the organisation's integrity, it also creates problems such as poor morale, lower production and higher turnover.

So ultimately, not being honest with one another also affects the overall performance of the organisation.

What does not come as a surprise is that in addition to the 'honesty' factor, the Florida State study also confirmed many earlier studies about the relationship between pay and turnover. It found that a good working environment is more important than pay and that "employees were more likely to leave if involved in an abusive relationship than if dissatisfied with pay".

The study did not suggest reasons for the high levels of dishonesty, merely the results. But could it be that honesty, particularly in western society, is in decline generally due to the emphasis on individualism not community? Have we become a 'me too' society, where material and personal gain are valued above the good of the community?

It seems that more and more, we read stories like Deutsche Telekom or hear of some new 'revelation' about a cover up, lack of integrity, or just plain dishonesty that has led to yet another major commercial or international disaster.

Has anything changed since 2008? It seems not. More recently, the Australian Royal Commission enquiry into the banking and financial services industry, has uncovered a raft of dishonesty amongst the industry leaders. As one press report commented "Financial giant AMP was wading knee-deep in blood on Tuesday as three more directors fell on their swords in the wake of damning revelations at the royal commission, including repeatedly lying to the regulator, deliberately ripping off customers and doctoring an 'independent report'." This board spill follows the resignation of the Chair, CEO and Chief Legal Officer just a week earlier. And this is but one example – other notable Australian financial organisations facing similar allegations include, The Commonwealth Bank of Australia, National Australia Bank, Westpac and ANZ – to name just a few.

Organisations, particularly since the late 80's, have spent an inordinate amount of time and resources on boosting the job 'satisfiers' (as Frederick Herzberg called them) – pay and conditions – at the expense of the true "motivators";

    WHAT TO DO WHEN LEADERSHIP IS NEEDED

- achievement,
- recognition for achievement,
- responsibility,
- meaningful and interesting work, and
- growth and advancement.

The result?

When material gain becomes the all-consuming and overt goal (such as maximum shareholder returns, exorbitant senior manager benefits, excessive incentive schemes for gaining new business) pursued by organisations over intrinsic basic human motivators, managers will do almost anything to 'cover their butt' so that their extrinsic rewards are maintained.

So, where does that leave today's managers? And, most importantly, what does it suggest for organisations that want to boost morale, increase productivity decrease staff turnover and be seen as more credible and trustworthy?

There are four things organisations should consider...

Firstly, the organisation needs to develop a culture of honesty. "It's OK to make mistakes and admit them." This philosophy must start from the board and the CEO. Organisational culture might seem like a 'soft' measure, yet it really is the glue that keeps the healthiest organisations performing well over the long term.

Secondly, regular reinforcement of shared values should occur through local workshops (team meetings) of all employees. These workshops should aim to discuss the key questions "What does our ideal organisation look like?" and "How do we (at our level) help the organisation move towards that ideal?"

Thirdly, the organisation needs to track progress towards its 'ideal' through both formal surveys and informal local workshops. Culture is something that needs to be continually reinforced and discussed at all levels – from the Board to the newest employee

And finally, and above all, managers need to be honest with what they say and do. A true manager's mantra should be "Do as I do", not "Do as I say".

People will accept mistakes if we are open about them. They will not accept cover-ups. The foundation for effective leadership and management is honesty. These are qualities that everyone values.

One final irony: Deutsche Telekom is the same company that (the previous year) pulled the plug on its sponsorship of the T-Mobile professional cycling team because of the sport's high-profile drug scandals!

"We arrived at this decision to separate our brand from further exposure from doping in sport and cycling specifically" said Deutsche Telekom Board member and CEO of T- Mobile International, Hamid Akhavan at the time.

"We have an obligation to our employees, customers and shareholders to focus our attention and resources on our core businesses."

Words say one thing – behaviour says another!

Personal leadership review and learning

1. What went well or not so well in these stories?
    *   What were the motivating factors behind the Deutsche Telekom decisions (spying on employees; withdrawing sport sponsorship), or perhaps the Australian banks and financial institutions (covering up 'independent reports', lying to customers and shareholders)?

2. At a personal level, what are the leadership lessons you can draw from these and other stories about honesty? (If you'd like to do a quick "self-assessment" of your honesty rating, complete the questionnaire on the following page).

3. What would I (or my organisation, my team) do differently in similar circumstances?
    *   Is there a culture of honesty in our organisation? In my team? How do I know?

     WHAT TO DO WHEN LEADERSHIP IS NEEDED

4. Is there something I now need to plan for as a result of this
   learning? If so, what?

Author's note

If you complete the 'Honesty Rating' on the following pages, transfer your thoughts about your results to the 'My Leadership Model' section at the end of the book.

Team Learning Exercise

The following exercise is one of the best I have encountered (the concept was given to me by my great mentor Dennis Pratt). It's called 'The Ideal Team' ('Team' can be substituted for 'Organisation' depending on your level and how you choose to use the exercise).

The basic principle behind this exercise enables it to be adapted to a variety of uses, such as improved customer service, production processes, marketing – in fact for any team or organisation that wishes to change and improve both the way it operates and the results it wants to achieve.

The Ideal Team

Distribute the story prior to a team meeting and ask everyone to read and answer the following two questions in Point 1. Head up your questions / discussion note with the title 'Our Ideal Team:':

1. Picture yourself working in your current role, in your current team –
   - What drives you to succeed at work? List as many things as possible that come to mind.
   - What are the aspects about your work (or place of work) that you value? (These questions should be sent as pre-work to the team members)

2. At the meeting, ask people to contribute points from their answers and draw up an agreed list of things that people like and share about the place of work and your team – these points in fact are your values.

3. Keeping in mind the work values you have just identified, develop
    a picture of your team as it might look if you could describe it to
    an outsider as 'my ideal team':
    - What do you want our team to look like in six months' time?
      This should be a team that will enable you to achieve your
      goals and provide job satisfaction.
    - What are the things that we can do (or not do, or perhaps
      stop doing) that will help make our team more like our ideal
      team?
    - What are those things that will work against the team
      moving towards our ideal?
    - From the list of things that we can do, reach agreement on
      the 3 or 4 most important things we must do to achieve this
      ideal team status.
    - On the other hand, what are the 2 or 3 things we must avoid
      doing if we are to achieve our ideal?

4. Develop an action plan to achieve your ideal team status. Make
    sure to include timelines and check points over the next six
    months to assess progress.

5. Finally, ask each team member to nominate publicly "The one most
    important thing I can do to help us become the ideal team is..."

Note: As you might expect from reading the above process, this
exercise will take longer than your normal team meeting. In fact you
may want to take your team off-site for a half-day meeting or use
it as the basis for a longer workshop. The results will be well worth
your time and effort.

Further suggested reading

Herzberg's Motivation Theory, Expert Program Management,
https://expertprogrammanagement.com/2018/04/herzbergs-two-
factor-theory/

Muth, M. & Selden, B., *Setting the Tone from the Top: How director
conversations shape culture*, AICD, 2017.

     WHAT TO DO WHEN **LEADERSHIP** IS NEEDED

Points to add to my Leadership Plan at the back of the
book:

My Honesty Rating

Rate yourself on the following aspects of honesty. Think about each statement, then give it a rating from 1 to 10 – "10" being "me at my best, all of the time" and "1" being "I need to improve dramatically on this aspect of honesty"	I rate my current status as...	New rating...
1. I keep my promises to the team		
2. I regularly give credit where it is due, when it is due		
3. I talk regularly with my people about their performance		
4. I talk regularly with my people about how they feel (not 'think') about their work		
5. I never invade the privacy of my people		
6. I do not take credit for the work of others		
7. I regularly report the good work of specific team members to my manager and other key stakeholders		
8. I only talk about the positive things one team member does when talking with other team members		
9. I encourage people to achieve to their full potential		
10. I only ask people to do things I would also do myself		
11. I give people increased responsibility as they develop in their role		
12. I provide people with the freedom to achieve agreed goals without looking over their shoulder		

13. I strive to make the work meaningful and interesting for my people		
14. I provide the opportunity for people to grow and develop		
15. I openly encourage people to admit their mistakes		
16. I treat mistakes as opportunities to develop, not to be punished		
17. I encourage my people to offer suggestions on how to improve work processes		
18. I encourage my people to offer suggestions on how to improve the way the team operates (the team process)		
19. I am aware of my three best strengths as a manager and the three areas I need to constantly address (my 'blind spots')		
20. I regularly encourage my people to provide me with feedback on my own performance		

If some of these scores were to move closer to 10 over the next three months, which would they be? Place your desired rating in the far column. Think about how you might achieve this new rating and record your thoughts in the 'My Leadership Model' at the end of the book.

DEVELOPING TRUST AND CREDIBILITY

11. WHAT'S YOUR BALANCE IN THE TRUST BANK?

- How to develop a culture of trust within the team

12. WHY LOYALTY PAYS

- How to develop a long-term strategy for building loyalty within your team

STORY 11:
14 MAY 2009

What's your balance in the Trust Bank?

Trust is a critical resource for organisations but is not always recognised as such. It is all too easy to forget that while trust takes a long time to build, the balance can be quickly depleted with just one careless withdrawal.

Chapter Objectives

- To develop a culture of trust within the team

Chapter theme

Catering for people's basic needs in challenging situations such as economic downturns or organisational crises, adds to a feeling of trust within all employees.

What's your balance in the Trust Bank?

There was a strange phenomenon happening in organisations around the globe during the GFC in 2008. And it's emblematic of what happens when any organisation is under external threat.

As the financial crisis first took hold, people gathered together and supported one another. It seemed that the usual response to an external threat was taking place, "We're being attacked. We're in this together and we can support one another through the difficulty."

The human instinct of fight or flight takes over. For example:

- There is more sharing of information and knowledge than usual to ensure everyone is 'being kept in the loop'.
- People go out of their way to find out what others are doing and how they can help.
- People are loyal to one another and particularly to those who might not be there at the moment (for example, on leave or assignment).
- People get together more at a social level (for example, business lunches are more common, although now much shorter and far less expensive as managers themselves tend to pay rather than the organisation).

That type of behaviour (pulling together against the external threat) may continue for some time. However, there's a change that takes place at a particular point. And that change seems to occur once there are lay-offs. As soon as people are laid off, the mood and the response from those that stay, changes:

- People become less sociable – lunches are definitely out, no matter who's paying.
- At the lower levels, individual employees start to emphasise (publicly) what they are achieving (sometimes even at the expense of colleagues) – people also 'spin the truth' to their advantage.
- On the other hand, some staff retreat into themselves and hope 'that it will all go away soon'.

     WHAT TO DO WHEN LEADERSHIP IS NEEDED

- Managers become less visible and remote. They are always in meetings. When asked about "What's happening?", very little of the real story emerges.
- There seem to be many things that are 'undiscussable'.

On the commercial front, organisations start cutting their marketing and training budgets – two of the most important items on any balance sheet. At the time of the GFC for instance, some organisations cut their marketing budget by as much as 70%. One wonders how much market share they had lost by the time the market started to pick up again.

Marketing brings in the business. Training helps to keep the people motivated and skilled, particularly on how to handle the business in these difficult times.

When dealing with external issues, organisations that are retreating and being negative rather than attacking and attempting to grow their market share also seem to be:

- Communicating with customers, suppliers and other key stakeholders more by email or text rather than face-to-face or phone. This is even more prevalent when they have bad news to give. And that's the worst way to give bad news.
- Treating suppliers and even customers, as somewhat alien rather than as business partners.

This approach hit home to a colleague who had been a trusted supplier to a firm for over 10 years – he even had his own log in code to enter the building for meetings. He told me that when he went to enter his code last week, it did not work. On enquiry, he was told that, "An instruction had gone out to the effect that no external providers be allowed direct access to the building".

As he said, "Having been around for many years, we've now seen the pendulum swing from contractors being considered business partners to now being viewed as recalcitrant, money-hungry, self-interested capitalists. I await with interest to see when the pendulum will start swinging back again! That's of course, if I'm still doing business with them."

The problem is, when the pendulum does start to swing back after the crisis, will a change in behaviour (towards the way it used to be) have any impact? Will people trust what others are now saying?

The late Steven Covey, in his '7 Habits of Highly Effective People' first introduced the notion of trust, not as a soft social virtue, but as a hard edged economic driver that can be deposited and withdrawn from one's emotional bank account. He suggested that it takes a long time to build up the trust balance by way of small deposits and this balance can be quickly depleted with just one withdrawal, such as in the above example with my colleague.

Trust is a critical resource in any market – be it bullish or recessionist. As Niklas Luhman (1979) found in his famous study on trust:

- Trust reduces the feeling of uncertainty.
- Trust makes a person feel more secure with regard to his or her acting (behaving, making decisions) or not acting.
- With trust, the person has the feeling of knowing what will happen in the future.
- Trust is used to lower the uncertainty regarding other people's behaviour.

So, managers - what to do in a tough environment? How to maintain trust with staff and other key stakeholders?

In tough times, people strive to satisfy their basic needs - food, shelter, security. However, people have little conscious awareness of these security needs except in times of emergency or periods of disorganisation. Famous psychologists such as Abraham Maslow and Frederick Hedrzberg, have demonstrated the need for people to satisfy their basic bodily needs before they can focus on higher needs such as achievement and self-actualisation.

As adults and parents however, we continually look to ensure these basic needs are satisfied for our children. Children often and openly display the signs of insecurity; the need for food; and the need to be safe, and we readily respond. Perhaps as we do with children, we also

   WHAT TO DO WHEN LEADERSHIP IS NEEDED

need to be more proactive and look for these signs in ourselves and others (yes, the behaviour is probably somewhat akin to 'childlike'), and readily respond to the need for food, shelter and security when times get tough.

So, when managing staff during challenging or even threatening times, whilst it's very important to share critical company information (which appeals to our higher needs of achievement and self-actualization), it's also very important to cater for people's basic needs. More socialising, interacting and even physical contact such as hand shaking, hugs etc. are needed. Some of you may have seen the news reports some time back of a man giving out 'free hugs' in New York. Many people were sceptical, but you could almost feel the positive energy from the people who were interviewed after experiencing a hug.

You'll note that such activities as socialising have been curtailed during the Covid crisis – for instance, how does one have a virtual handshake? What can organisations do to maintain the need for socialising, whilst maintaining social distancing? These are real challenges for organisations, as people's basic needs must be met, despite the situation.

As an example of effective socialising, one colleague who works in the construction industry, which was experiencing a particularly challenging time, took his four direct reports to the football - a first for him and the firm. The mood and particularly collaboration within his team, improved dramatically afterwards. Another colleague, when her firm was about to be faced by a particularly challenging external audit, for the three weeks prior to the audit, placed a bowl of fruit on the staff lunch room table each day and once a week a small bowl of sweets – although only a small gesture, the conversation around this action was uplifting for all.

And the same is true for other stakeholders such as customers and suppliers. In challenging situations, will you do more face-to-face or phone communication rather than email, so that you can address basic personal needs?

Cost pressures have led to many face-to-face meetings being replaced with teleconferencing, with varying degrees of success. Teleconferencing can be extremely effective for discussing the key business issues. However, how do you handle the necessary social interaction? How do people build the essential social and emotional bonds required to cement lasting deals? How do you have a virtual meal, drink, tea/coffee together?

And what happens after the meeting?

Experience suggests that there are often 'meetings after meetings' (particularly after tele-meetings) where small local groups gather (generally over tea or coffee, or in the case of Covid, by phone) to discuss what was really said or meant in the meeting and by whom.

How will your product or service (or perhaps the way you deliver these) help satisfy your key stakeholder's basic needs for safety and security? You may recall my earlier story of how Hyundai dramatically increased their market share in the US during the GFC by applying this basic principle of catering to people's need for security rather than thinking of their own drive to increase sales.

The message?

As a manager working with staff and other stakeholders, when times are tough:

- Look for ways to increase social contact
- Search for options that will satisfy people's need for safety and security
- Be prepared to spend more face-to-face time with key people
- Be prepared to discuss the 'undiscussable' (if you don't, others certainly will, and often negatively)

People can only do their best work when their basic needs are catered and cared for. Customers and suppliers can only be true business partners when they feel safe and secure working with you. Shareholders will only support board decisions when they believe the company is in safe hands, In challenging situations or tightening economic times, it's important to stress security, food and shelter

 WHAT TO DO WHEN LEADERSHIP IS NEEDED

before talking about business performance. It's important to build your level of trust deposits with the people that are important to your success.

Personal leadership review and learning

1. What went well or not so well in these stories?
    - The issue of trust is a basic, yet critical factor that managers should always consider. Is trust an issue within your team or organisation at the moment? What has happened to 'trust' in your organisation post-Covid?

2. At a personal level, what are the leadership lessons you can draw from this and other stories about trust?

3. What would I (or my organisation, my team) do differently in similar circumstances?
    - What do you need to reinforce when people's basic needs are threatened?

4. Is there something I now need to plan for as a result of this learning? If so, what?

Author's note

Although this story was originally written in May 2009 at the height of the impact of the GFC, there are still the same issues evident today around the globe, particularly after the Covid-19 lockdowns experienced in many countries.

One of the key foundations of leadership is to ensure people's basic needs – i.e. food, shelter, social and security – are met. It's only when people feel safe and secure in their environment that they can give of their best.

The important point to remember is that when these basic needs are threatened, people turn in on themselves, they lose trust in others.

It's also interesting to note that the same behaviours people adopt in times of stress as caused by the GFC or the Covid pandemic for example, are exactly the same behaviours displayed during mergers and takeovers, i.e.

- People become less sociable.
- At the lower levels, staff start to emphasise (publicly) what they are achieving (sometimes even at the expense of colleagues) – people also 'spin the truth' to their advantage.
- Some staff retreat into themselves and hope "that it will all go away soon".
- Managers become less visible and remote. They are always in meetings. When
- asked about "What's happening?", very little of the real story emerges.
- There seem to be many things that are 'undiscussable'.

Remember, the Trust Bank is open all hours for deposits – and withdrawals!

Team Learning Exercise

Developing trust within a team takes time. One of the best foundations for building trust, is to start discussing the issue. Here's a suggested way you might use this trust story with your team.

1. Distribute the story prior to a team meeting and ask everyone to read and answer the following questions (as usual, feel free to pick and choose the questions, or add your own):
    - What are the indicators in our organisation that there is a good level of trust?
    - What indicators are there that might indicate trust is at risk? (e.g. How are people treated when they leave, retire, are fired, or made redundant? Or, how are people treated when they make mistakes? Or, how is conflict managed within the team?)
    - What can you do at a personal level to ensure, or further develop trust within our team?
    - What do you think others should do? Why?

2. At the meeting decide which questions if answered well, will be most beneficial to the team.

 WHAT TO DO WHEN LEADERSHIP IS NEEDED

3. Lead a discussion on the selected questions to reach consensus on:
    - What action needs to be taken?
    - By whom?
    - By when?
    - How will our results be measured? When?

Further suggested reading

Covey, S. *Seven Habits of Highly Effective People*, Free Press 2004.

Points to add to my Leadership Plan at the back of the book:

STORY 12:
10 JAN 2008

Why loyalty pays

Loyalty is something that seems to have been lost in many modern organisations. Corporate decision- makers seem to think that paying people more will gain their loyalty. It does not. All it gains is their compliance. And there's a huge difference between 'loyalty' and 'compliance'.

Chapter Objectives

- How to develop a long term strategy for building loyalty within your team

Chapter theme

Loyalty builds through relationships, not salary, pay or incentives.

Why Loyalty Pays

In 2008 Tata Motors released the revolutionary "Nano" in India, the world's cheapest car - $2,500!

What's that got to do with loyalty you may well ask? Well, the CEO of Tata, Ratan Tata, aged 70 who took over the ailing company business in 1991, has a personal mantra of "loyalty". He is unusual for a CEO. Tata is humble, openly admitting his mistakes and sends personal "thank you" notes to employees. In a recent deal with terminated workers from his steel company, he agreed to pay their wages for life!

When Ratan Tata took over as Chairman of the group, he was forced to earn rather than command respect - he inherited Tata through his mother's marriage, not blood lines. At that time the company was a loose knit group, dependent purely on the Indian economy and not performing well. Today, it is a major international player. It now owns many diverse international businesses ranging from one of the biggest world steel makers, Corus Steel in the UK to the prestigious Ritz Carlton in Boston – it also owns Jaguar and Land Rover. The Tata group now has market capitalisation of $70 billion and after tax profit of $2.8 billion.

Ratan Tata's gentle, kind manner engenders loyalty and yet he encourages his managers to make tough decisions. "Mr Tata encourages us to take big, calculated risks," said Ravi Kant, Tata Motors' Managing Director at the unveiling of the Nano. His style appears to be the ultimate "tough mind, gentle hand" approach.

Unfortunately, loyalty is a philosophy that seems to have been lost in many modern organisations. Powerful corporate decision makers seem to think that paying people more salary and perks will gain their loyalty. It does not. All it gains is their compliance. So when people are offered more money, because they have no loyalty to the organisation, they quickly and easily change companies.

Compare this with two other examples.

As a management coach, I was working with a mid-level executive who was told six months ago that her division was likely to be closed down at Christmas. As the company wanted to keep her, this timing gave her the opportunity to seek a role elsewhere in the company. Unfortunately, there were no suitable roles. So, the company has now instigated termination.

Now here's the "loyalty" kicker. As well as a very generous termination package, her salary will continue to be paid for the next nine months. During this time, she is encouraged to remain at work. Should she happen to find a role outside the company at any time within the next nine months, as an additional "thank you", the company will continue to pay her 50% of her current salary for the remainder of the nine months. She has just found a new role and starts in two week's time. Can you imagine how fondly she talks of her old employer and of the level of "loyalty" credibility that has been built up by the company with their existing employees?

Closer to home, my wife worked for a very successful European major multinational pharmaceutical company. They have tremendous loyalty amongst their employees with many of them being lifetime employees. What engenders such loyalty? Well, in addition to good leadership and management, loyalty starts with the employment contract. Both parties are required to give six month's notice of leaving or termination.

Faced with an unexpected termination, would you rather be given the option of a six months window to find a new role, or the ignominy, embarrassment and belittlement of being marched off the premises by armed security guards on the day of termination?

Just as importantly, what "loyalty" impact does each of these termination decisions have on those employees who stay?

Loyalty is a two-way street. It cannot be bought. It must be earned – by managers and employees. Loyalty may well cost - most often in the time invested in people by the organisation's leaders - but it also pays. In spades!

     WHAT TO DO WHEN LEADERSHIP IS NEEDED

Personal leadership review and learning

1. What are the lessons about loyalty from these different events and experiences? Most importantly, what's the one consistent theme?
   - To many older managers, loyalty seems a thing of the past. What can managers and staff do in the current environment to engender a sense of loyalty?

2. At a personal level, what are the leadership lessons you can draw from this and other stories about loyalty?

3. This is a good news story. What can I (or my organization, my team) do differently (or keep doing) to help develop loyalty? For instance:
   - What should I do more of?
   - What should I do less of?
   - What should I keep doing?

4. Is there something I now need to plan for as a result of this learning? If so, what?

Author's note

As you can see, this story was written some years ago. Since then, we've had the full impact of the GFC with organisations looking everywhere to cut costs. Many of the cost cutting messages have been by way of the employment contract – there seem to be fewer and fewer employment contracts these days.

Companies are tending to hire more casual and temporary staff rather than full time staff so that they can remain more flexible.
- What does such an approach do to loyalty?
- Can an organisation engender a culture of loyalty under these changed circumstances?

A post script: Oh, and by the way, the organisation my wife worked for went through a merger about three years ago. There's been a 'new way of doing things' introduced. Employment contracts have changed with only 'highly valued' employees getting the six month termination clause. A new performance management system forces managers to rate and distribute their people's performance in terms of the bell shaped curve ('calibration' they call it). Many loyal people have left and the feeling of loyalty to the organisation has diminished (although there still seems to be a culture of loyalty to the local team). However, one wonders how long this will last under the 'new way of doing things'.

Team Learning Exercise:

Loyalty is a long-term strategy – it will not happen overnight. You should consider this before running a team meeting on the subject. For this reason, the following team meeting exercise is quite different to some others in this book.

1. Distribute the story prior to a team meeting and ask everyone to read and answer the following questions:
    - Assume that it is now ..../.........................../................... (Place a date at least three years into the future here).
    - Over the last three years the people have developed a real sense of loyalty to the organisation and to one another.
    - What did we as an organisation do to develop this feeling of loyalty?
    - What did we as a team do to develop this feeling of loyalty?
    - What did I personally do to develop this feeling of loyalty?
    - To achieve this great feeling of loyalty there were a number of obstacles to overcome. What were they?
    - How did we overcome these obstacles? What did we do?

2. At the meeting, ask people to list the things that the organisation, the team and they personally have done over the three years to develop a feeling of loyalty. You should list and categorise these under three separate headings, "Organisation", "Our Team". "Me". Make sure people continue to talk as if they are in the future, three years from now. Keep stating we are now in (the year), what have we done over the last three years?

3. Starting with the points under "Me", lead a discussion to agree:
    - What each of us can do . . .
        » more of
        » less of, or
        » keep doing, to engender loyalty.

 WHAT TO DO WHEN LEADERSHIP IS NEEDED

4. During the discussion, when people start to get off the track or become somewhat negative (e.g. "That won't work around here"), remind them that we are now three years into the future – nothing's happened yet, we'll deal with barriers shortly.

5. Move on to cover "Our Team"- many of these points will have now been discuss under "Me", so just confirm – no need to repeat.

6. Finally, move to a discussion on "Organisation". The organisation points may be a little difficult to implement, so people should focus on how to influence others to implement these.

7. Now's the time to discuss the barriers to achieving loyalty. Some of these will be able to be handled by you and the team. As with previous meetings, the team will need to decide:
    - What action needs to be taken?
    - By whom?
    - By when?
    - How will our results be measured? When?

    Some barriers may be outside of the team, individual or even your control. You will need to state this and decide what you will do to try to influence change within the organisation.

Further suggested reading

This one is unusual for me, as I have no 'Further suggested reading' – I couldn't come across a text or article that fits with my views on the subject. For example when I Googled 'Building loyalty in an organisation', eight of the nine links on page one, listed 'customer loyalty', 'brand loyalty', or 'business market loyalty'. Only one reference referred to employees, and then it only covered such superfluous (and in my opinion, erroneous) tips such as "Have a proper chain of command and an open door policy". Should you know of a good reference, please send me the details.

Points to add to my Leadership Plan at the back of the book:

WHAT TO DO WHEN LEADERSHIP IS NEEDED

MANAGING
STAKEHOLDERS

13. *FIFTEEN YEARS IN THE MAKING*
- How to identify your six key stakeholders
- How to write a "statement of intent" for each stakeholder group

STORY 13:
22 JULY 2011

15 Years in the making!

At the time of the recession (GFC) we found ourselves in something that was inevitable – it had been brewing for the previous 15 years. Why? Because investing had been replaced by short-term trading and the interests of shareholders and senior staff had been placed above those of other stakeholders.

Chapter Objectives

- How to identify your six key stakeholders

- How to write a "statement of intent" for each stakeholder group

Chapter theme

Organisational structure and its importance to the team's purpose and strategic direction.

15 Years In The Making!

Actually, it probably started a little earlier than 15 years ago. In 1974 the US Securities and Exchange Commission introduced deregulation of brokerage commission costs. Prior to this, it would cost a broker or trader approximately $1 commission per traded share. Today that figure is somewhat like $0.01 per share. So, one can readily see that trading in shares today is a far less expensive way to bolster one's finances than it was all those years ago.

"So, what's been 15 years coming? It's the recession (2010). A recession we had to have. But what has that got to do with the cost of share trading? And why did it have to happen?"

Approximately fifteen years earlier the internet really took off. People could now not only communicate instantly across the globe, but they could also do most, if not all, financial transactions without leaving their desk (or home for that matter).

Combine the two facts – negligible commission costs on trading of shares and the ability to trade shares on line – and you suddenly have a new industry, share trading. Note; this is 'share trading' not investing. Gone are the days when people made investments for something they believed in, it was now "how much can we make on each trade?"

Prior to 1974, you needed a broker to buy or sell shares for you. Now everyone, you and I included, can trade shares. It's no longer only people genuinely investing in companies for long-term benefit (their own and the company's) - it's how much money we can make in the shortest possible time.

Given this, it's easy to see why CEOs have been set targets that are at a minimum double digit annual increase return on investment (ROI is one key indicator that influences share price), and rather than annual reports, companies are now judged on quarterly results. Shares even move up or down based on a company's projected earnings for the next quarter.

So, why did such changes eventually lead to a recession (between 2008 and 2010)?

Organisational development practitioner, Dennis Pratt, suggests that every organisation public or private, large or small - has six key stakeholders:

- customers,
- suppliers,
- owners,
- staff,
- industry and
- the community.

Whenever the needs of one or more of these stakeholder groups are consistently exceeded at the expense of the needs of the other stakeholders, the focus of the organisation changes and can ultimately lead to its downfall.

So, if that happens to a number of organisations within the one industry sector, say finance and banking, then the entire industry may crash. As finance and banking is such a pivotal industry in our economic community, its crash at the time led to crashes in other industries (such as housing and motor manufacturing to name just two). Ultimately, we have a recession. In the 2008-10 recession, the two stakeholder groups whose needs were focused on at the expense of others, were shareholders and senior staff.

Today, shareholders are no longer 'shareholders' in the true sense of the word – people who have a genuine interest in the long-term benefit of the company, i.e. 'owners' who 'hold' shares. Shareholders today for the most part, are made up of institutions (investment funds, pension funds etc. – these are the large 'traders') together with the small traders, the people who are trading shares, often online.

While those who trade in shares may argue "Yes, but we also look closely at the fundamentals of the company as a guide to investing", they will also readily admit that they follow the market, industry sector and company trends to buy and sell irrespective of their genuine interest in a particular company. It's all about making money in the shortest possible time.

   WHAT TO DO WHEN LEADERSHIP IS NEEDED

Testament to this is the strategy of buying or selling short, which was banned in some countries for a period, as it is a genuine form of gambling. For example, in 2008 the US Securities and Exchange Commission banned what it called "abusive naked short selling" as a method of driving down share prices.

Short selling also fell under heavy scrutiny during the global financial crisis when Australia, Canada and several European nations placed bans on short selling of financial stocks. Since that time, regulations have been lifted or amended in some countries, but generally speaking the United States has more liberal laws on short selling than most of the world.

Such moves are government attempts to reign in the excesses of these two stakeholder groups – shareholders (traders) and senior executive staff. But is it too little too late?

An article at the time highlighted the issue. The International Herald Tribune, (June 9th 2009) talked about the staff stakeholder excesses: "In the past, banks had free reign to determine the base salaries and bonuses they gave their employees. When the economy was riding high, bonuses for top Wall Street executives and traders soared to tens of millions of dollars. Critics say the bonuses often encouraged risk-taking, since star bankers could walk away with huge amounts of money, even if bets they took failed to take off." (Note the use of the word "bets" in this article)

The US government (like governments elsewhere) commenced proposing guidelines to curb executive pay. The regulations passed by Congress limits bonuses of the top 25 executives to no greater than a third of their salary. The problem is, these executives are not likely to be subject to a salary cap. The legislation ends up being meaningless. And as for guidelines – who is likely to follow them?

In other countries, legislation has been passed to have shareholders monitor the salaries and bonuses of senior executives. For example, in Australia the Australian Corporations Act, states that if 25% or more of votes cast at two consecutive AGMs oppose the adoption of a remuneration report (for senior executive salary and bonuses), then the company must formally respond by asking all board members (except the managing director) to stand for re-election within 90 days. In addition, key management personnel whose remuneration is disclosed in the remuneration report are excluded from voting, ensuring those with an obvious interest in the outcome cannot vote.

However, to me these types of regulations do not address the issue. It still leaves the decision with the two most powerful stakeholder groups – owners and staff. After all, if the company is doing well and share prices are high, why would shareholders want to curb executive pay? It's in their best interests to keep the staff stakeholder happy.

In the case of legislation (such as that in Australia), it only appears to bite when something goes wrong – either the share price takes a major dive, or the executives are found to be undertaking illegal or fraudulent practices (as happened in May 2018 when the Australian Royal Commission Enquiry into the banking and financing industry, forced many board members and senior executives to lose their jobs).

These methods appear to be retrospective rather than proactive. So what's the answer?

First, a new approach to executive compensation - fairness and equity for all those included in the staff stakeholder group, from the CEO to the newest hire - is needed. Such an approach would be based on;

- fixed salary,
- organisation success,
- team success, and
- personal performance.

These would be in descending order of value, so that the largest portion of pay would be salary, with the smallest, personal performance. Implementing this would ensure that the staff stakeholder needs are met, not consistently exceeded.

Turning to the shareholder stakeholder group, they are now no longer owners, rather traders. We cannot return to the pre – 1970's.

So, why not have two classes of shareholder? The first class would be those who trade shares over the short term. They would be ineligible to vote as shareholders. In the strictest definition of the term, these traders are not part of the shareholder group anyway, they are more like suppliers providing capital to the organisation.

The second class would be those who hold the shares for a minimum of two years. They would have full shareholder voting rights and be "owners" in the true sense of the word as they have shown a long term interest in the company. In this way, CEOs would have to answer to genuine owners, not fly-by-night gamblers.

As a result of the recession, the community stakeholder now has a voice that is being listened to more closely and more often. It's up to you and I as part of the community stakeholder, to suggest ways to our politicians that will ensure there is a balance between the needs of all six organisational stakeholders.

Personal leadership review and learning

1. What can we learn about salaries, incentives and bonuses from this story?
    - Does money per se, motivate people?

2. At a personal level, what are the leadership lessons you can draw from this and other stories about loyalty?

3. What can I (or my organization, my team) do differently (or keep doing) to encourage motivation within the workforce? For instance:
    - What should I do more of?
    - What should I do less of?
    - What should I keep doing?

4. Is there something I now need to plan for as a result of this learning? If so, what?

Author's note

In this story, the three principle stakeholders mentioned are the owners, staff and the community. Each organisation, group or team has in fact six stakeholder groups that they need to manage:

The organisation must answer the question
"How do we <u>intend</u> to be seen by each of these stakeholders?"

The secret to successful stakeholder management is to do five things:

1. Identify who makes up each of the six stakeholder groups for your team (actually name them).

2. Develop a "Statement of Intent" – i.e. "How do we intend to be seen by each of these stakeholder groups?" (your statement will be specific for each group)

3. Assess how you are currently seen by each stakeholder group. You may even do a survey, or interview some of these stakeholders to assess your current standing.

4. Develop a plan for managing each stakeholder group (i.e. how do you plan to achieve your Statement of Intent? How are you currently seen? What do you need to do to bridge the gap or maintain the status quo?

5. Regularly review both your Statement of Intent and how well you are achieving this by your stakeholder management policies and strategies.

 WHAT TO DO WHEN LEADERSHIP IS NEEDED

Team Learning Exercise

This exercise is one of the more critical ones for your team as it will set the direction you wish to go. It should even be the starting point for the development of your strategic plan. As such, you will need to set aside some considerable time for this meeting – a minimum of half a day is required and my experience suggests that a one-day workshop is best.

1. Distribute the story prior to a team meeting including a copy of the Stakeholder Map. Ask everyone to read and answer the following questions and bring their answers to the workshop (For this meeting, please stick to the script – this process has been used by me for more than twenty years and really does work):

    - Take a large sheet of paper (A3 is ideal). Write the name of your team in the centre.
    - Who are the people, departments, organisations that you deal with that may have an impact on your success? Write their names around the outside of the page and draw a line to the centre (your team's name). These may include, but are not limited to:
        » your customers – if more than one, name them – if you have a large group, name that group,
        » your suppliers - i.e. those that provide you with the resources – physical and advice – to enable you to do your work,
        » the staff – people who work with you and perhaps report to you,
        » the industry – these will include your competitors, industry groups, government bodies etc. that play a part in your industry,
        » the owners – if you are an internal team, this will be senior management (representing shareholders) or if you are the executive team, these will be the actual shareholders,
        » the community – these may be local neighbours, social groups, lobby groups/organisations.

» If you've not already done so, group these people into the six stakeholder groups in the form of a map – you may need to take a clean sheet to complete this.

- On another sheet of paper, take each group in turn and complete a Statement of Intent – i.e. "How do we (as a team) intend to be seen by each?"

2. At the meeting start by having a general discussion around the article - focus this discussion on the stakeholder concept. Then draw up a large Stakeholder Map on a Whiteboard. Ask people to start giving you their stakeholders and through discussion, draw up a Stakeholder Map for your team.

3. Lead a discussion to develop a Statement of Intent for each stakeholder group (if you have a large team, you may split the team up so that sub groups take one or two stakeholders each to report back to the main team). Remember, the aim is to answer the question (for each stakeholder), "How do we intend to be seen?"

4. Through plenary discussion, reach consensus on a Statement of Intent for each stakeholder group.
Note: Try not to dwell too much on getting the words exactly right – someone can take the general statements away and tidy them up after the meeting.

5. You may continue now to develop plans for managing each group, or set aside time for another meeting to conclude the exercise. Main points to cover are:
   - How are we currently seen by each stakeholder group?
   - What action needs to be taken to close any gap to achieve our Statement of Intent or maintain the status quo?
   - By whom?
   - By when?
   - How will our results be measured? When?

Further suggested reading

For an interesting discussion on this topic go to Destination Innovation *"Who are a Company's most important Stakeholders?"* https://www.destination- innovation.com/who-are-a-companys-most-important-stakeholders/#comment-24224

Points to add to my Leadership Plan at the back of the book:

BUILDING A TEAM OR A GROUP

14. TOUR DE FARCE OR TEAM DE FORCE?

- How to generate cooperation and collaboration within the group or team

STORY 14:
1 AUGUST 2008

Tour de Farce or Team de Force?

Do you manage a team or a group? The distinction is an important one, because there's no point in trying to develop a team ethos amongst a group of people who do not really need to work together as a team.

Chapter Objectives

- To develop activities, behaviours and actions that will engender cooperation and collaboration within the group or team.

Chapter theme

Distinguishing between a 'group' and a 'team' can provide managers with a far more focused way in which they approach the development of 'teamwork'.

Tour de Farce or Team de Force?

It's probably fair to say that most followers and even casual observers of the Tour de France of 2008 expected the race to throw up (no pun intended) some drug cheats. True to form, we were not disappointed, with four riders failing drug tests and being disqualified (not to mention being unceremoniously taken away from their team buses by the French police!).

But the race also threw up an interesting question. Why did the teams of the first two disqualified riders continue in the race, while another, Sunier Duval-Scott, withdraw all their riders? Commentators and keen followers of the sport were divided as to whether the first two teams, while not legally obliged to do so, were morally obliged to withdraw.

But there might be another angle to this question.

Cycling is often seen as an individual sport – to the uninitiated it appears as if it's 'everyone for himself'. In fact, one of the most often asked questions by the uninitiated is "How can one person be helped by his team mates when they are all on separate bikes?"

As in key businesses, the answer of course is teamwork; in particular, dependence on one another for success. For example in cycling, good teams protect their key riders by allowing them to draft along in the pack out of harm's way. Various team members will also take the lead in the pack at certain times to either slow or speed up the race to suit their key riders.

The best three teams on the 2008 tour in terms of overall results were Garmin, CSC and Columbia. It is commonly known that they also had the best morale, friendship and motivation. Interestingly, these three teams were the only ones with independent (and extremely costly) drug testing regimes.

Whilst these three teams are truly multinational, the members of these teams are all great mates. Their on-the-road performances were superb - perhaps largely due to their trust in and dependence on each other.

     WHAT TO DO WHEN LEADERSHIP IS NEEDED

And with the testing of every single aspect of their health, there would be no way of cheating whilst in these teams – therefore 100% confidence by their fellow team mates and their bosses.

Compare this with the reports on some of the other teams where there is often a split within the team along nationality or language lines (often English, Spanish and Italian).

My contention is that the successful teams are just that, 'teams', whereas those less successful operate as 'groups'. The way teams and groups operate and are managed is quite different.

So, as managers, do you have a team or a group?

Many managers waste a lot of time trying to develop team work amongst a group of people reporting to them who do not have any need to work cooperatively together, or form up as a team. They all have different functions and they don't rely on each other to achieve their individual results.

In sport for instance, some Olympic 'teams' are in fact groups, where the success of one member does not impact the success of others. For example, swimming has individual events where one member of the national 'team' can be a champion, winning many medals, yet the overall 'team' results are poor (by comparison to other national 'teams').

So, what's the difference between a group and a team?

Groups are formed by at least two people who interact and may share some interrelated task goals. However, the majority of the work group members undertake can be done without relying on other members of the group.

For example, often the 'top team' of the organisation is in fact a group rather than a team. The members each have a defined area of responsibility – perhaps they all contribute to the broad goal of 'organisation success' and perhaps there are elements of collaboration required to achieve that broad goal – but most of their own function may be successfully managed without having to rely on all of the other 'top team' members. A similar example may be sales 'teams' where sales people are all selling the same product and are allocated to regions, areas or departments. Individual sales people can achieve highly successful results without having to rely on other sales people for their support.

Teams on the other hand, are groups that have three additional characteristics that set them apart:

1. Their members must depend on one another to achieve their task goals.
2. Each member must have a particular role to play in the team.
3. There must be team goals and objectives that can only be achieved by all the team members contributing to a total team output.

So in a team, if one member doesn't fulfill his or her role, it's not just that person's own functional area that fails, the whole team fails. This is not the case within a group.

In sport, two good examples of where true teams are required, are cricket and baseball. In both sports, every member has to be able to bat – the team goal is to score more runs than the opposition; every member has to be able to throw and catch a ball – they must all have at least a basic level of hand/eye coordination. The team goal is to restrict the opposition to as few runs as possible; and some members, as well as being able to bat, throw and catch, need to have specialist skills if the team is to be successful. In baseball, for example, it's the pitcher and catcher; in cricket it's the bowler and wicket keeper.

In both games, teams can only be successful when every member of the team feels confident that he or she can rely on every other member of the team to make a competent contribution and do his or her job well.

So does your situation call for team work or group work? As a manager, the consequences of making that decision, can greatly impact your time management. Teams are likely to take more time initially to develop team work. However, once they are working well, they can become almost self-managing.

It also impacts a manger's style of communication. In a group, the manager will need to do far more one-on-one communicating – his/her style can also be more varied depending on the needs of the situation and the personality of the particular group member. With teams, there will be far more one-to-team and intra-team communication – his/her style will need to be far more collaborative (if not, morale and motivation are likely to drop off).

Finally, it has obvious implications for 'team building' initiatives. With groups, efforts should be more directed to social interaction – collaboration will be built through personal relationships, not the dependence on one another for results. With teams, more time will be spent in problem-solving, team building exercises and team role definitions.

The 2008 Tour de France provided us with a very strong message for managers. The team that had the best results – CSC – with overall winner, best young rider and best team - showed true team work throughout the race. People helped one another, leadership was shared - even the most experienced of commentators could not tell you who the team leader was until very late in the race.

In fact, the leadership of the team changed throughout the race with quite a number of members taking on the role as the situation demanded. Noted leadership writer Charles Handy would have been proud to see his 'distributed leadership' model being played out so successfully in the World's biggest annual sporting event.

So if you have the responsibility for managing the performance of a group of other people, it may be time to consider the question – "Do I have a group or a team?"

Personal leadership review and learning

1. Having read this story, do you believe you are managing a group or a team? Perhaps you have a combination (quite often possible in matrix organisations – however, the rules of managing each still apply, so be careful to manage each a little differently).

2. At a personal level, what are the leadership lessons you can draw from this and your personal experiences about working in groups and teams?

3. This is a good news story. What can I (or my organization, my team) do differently (or keep doing) to help develop a feeling of team? For instance:
   - What should I do more of?
   - What should I do less of?
   - What should I keep doing?

4. Is there something I now need to plan for as a result of this learning? If so, what?

Author's note:

The distinction between a team and a group is important for it will influence the way you manage your people. Members of both are required to interact with one another quite differently as shown in the following diagram:

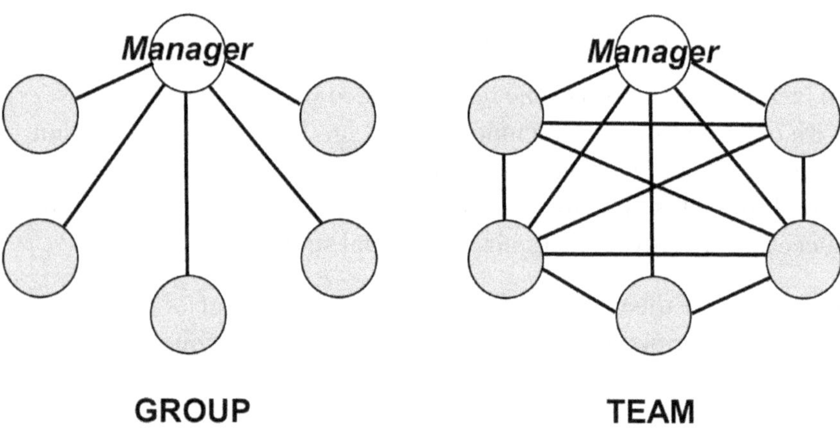

 WHAT TO DO WHEN LEADERSHIP IS NEEDED

Characteristics of Groups	Characteristics of Teams
✓ Individual accountability – members are primarily concerned with achieving their own objectives.	✓ Accountability – whilst individual members have specific objectives, they are primarily concerned with the contribution of those objectives to achieving the team's goals.
✓ Group leadership is generally through positional authority (e.g. the manager, CEO, etc.).	✓ Team leadership may initially be through positional authority (e.g. manager) but at times can also be taken by other members (e.g. project teams) or handed over by the manager for specific tasks (e.g. problem solving meetings).
✓ Groups will sometimes work collaboratively, but members put their own objectives foremost.	✓ Members work collaboratively and respect other team members because they need to achieve common goals and objectives.
✓ Often the manager determines and plans the work of his/her group members and the jobs are narrowly defined.	✓ In the team environment the manager often collaborates with members as a peer and jointly establishes and plans the work.

Team Learning Exercise

Spending time in trying to develop a group (who are a genuine 'group') into a 'team' with various 'team building exercises' can at best be a waste of time for the manager, and at worst can be seen by the 'group' as artificial or even hypocritical.

1. Distribute the story prior to your meeting and ask everyone to read and answer the following questions (as usual, feel free to pick and choose the questions, or add your own):
    * What distinguishes a team from a group? How and where can each work successfully? Why? Examples?
    * What are the indicators in our group that suggest that we are either a 'group' or a 'team'? Why?
    * What types of activities are best suited to support cohesiveness, cooperation, and ultimately success in:
        * a team?
        * a group?
    * What can you do at a personal level to provide support to your colleagues and to your manager?
    * What support do you suggest your manager (and/or the organisation) provide to boost collaboration and morale?

2. At the meeting decide which questions if answered well, will be most beneficial to the team.

3. Lead a discussion on the selected questions to reach consensus on:
    * What action needs to be taken?
    * By whom?
    * By when?
    * How will our results be measured? When?

Further suggested reading

Ribeiro, S., May 1, 2020 *Workplace Collaboration: Team vs Group,* Flockblog
https://blog.flock.com/workplace-collaboration-teams-vs-groups

Points to add to my Leadership Plan at the back of the book:

THE LEADERSHIP ASPECTS OF *PEOPLE* MANAGEMENT

15. THE AGING WORKFORCE – DISAPPEARING ASSET?

- How to use the knowledge and skills of older workers

16. CAN YOU REALLY WORK FROM ANYWHERE?

- How to manage work from home versus office

17. IS BUSINESS ACUMEN A SUBSTITUTE FOR LEADERSHIP?

- How to develop business, people, and strategic management skills

STORY 15:
21 MARCH 2008

The aging workforce – a disappearing asset?

For as long as I can remember, commentators have suggested that all organisations should consider people their "greatest asset". In the boom years of the 1980s and the 90s, this thinking literally translated to 'pay people more and we will keep them'. But today, despite higher salaries and benefits, we find people change employers quite regularly. Why?

Chapter Objectives

- To classify the skills and characteristics older employees can bring to the workplace.

- To identify the part older employees can play in the local team or group, and throughout the organisation.

- To identify roles that former or older employees can fulfill.

Chapter theme

Building on the experience of long-term employees and/or older employees and recognizing how the team can use their knowledge, skills and organisational maturity.

The aging workforce – a disappearing asset?

Statistics on change of employer over a working lifetime are hard to come by – estimates range between three and seven. The key point, however, is that people are now far more willing to change employers than ever before.

Not only do people change jobs more readily, but the workforce is aging. Figures in the US suggest that the average working age is now 42 up from 35 in 1980. By 2015, according to the American Association of Retired Persons, one of every five employees was at least 55.

In the UK, the combination of declining birth rates and greater longevity means that by 2030 the number of people aged 50 and over will have reached 46 per cent of the total UK population, rising from 33 per cent in 2002.

These trends are also evident in other developed countries such as France, Germany, Spain and Japan.

An aging population means more people leaving the workforce for retirement. On the other hand, the number of older people who work part-time is also increasing.

These trends represent two challenges for organisations. Firstly, how do we keep our best, most experienced and knowledgeable people? And secondly, how do we make better use of those who are considering retirement?

The answer to the first question is simple (although implementing it may be more challenging). Treat people better, engage them fully and develop employee loyalty. It is long past due that organisations realise that treating people as 'their greatest assets', means more than traditional financial asset management through pay and benefits.

Keeping older people employed - and thus reducing staff turnover rates - delivers an immediate financial benefit. But more than this, studies also suggest that older people are better workers.

For example, the Canadian Centre for Occupational Health and Safety report that older workers exhibit lower turnover, more

 WHAT TO DO WHEN LEADERSHIP IS NEEDED

dedication to the workplace, and have more positive work values. Absenteeism is less frequent, although it is longer when it does happen.

The answer to the second challenge – making better use of older workers – is already being met by some organisations. Can we take a lead from the following three examples?

In 1989 the UK DIY retailer B&Q opened an outlet in Macclesfield. The new store enjoyed low turnover of staff, low levels of absenteeism, high profits and soon established a positive image in the local community. It was also staffed entirely by over 50s. The success of this organisational experiment encouraged the company to develop its over 50s recruitment policy. It now boasts that of a total staff of 37,000, 22 per cent are over 50.

Further, The Chicago Transit Authority implemented a Phase-In Retirement program for retiring employees. This program gradually acclimatises mature workers to retirement by steadily reducing their work hours and pay rates, but concurrently gives them their pensions. Older workers are also encouraged to become mentors for younger employees.

The third example comes from Hewlett Packard which has found a new resource – loyal former employees. HP has an army of former employees who often give their time voluntarily as marketers, good-will ambassadors and in-store sales people.

Enlightened organisations such as these are now re-employing former workers either full time or part time to take advantage of their expertise and in many cases, their desire to stay actively engaged in the workforce.

However, to take advantage of the aging workforce, organisations need to treat their existing employees (both young and old) as more than merely 'assets'. Long term loyalty can only be gained through a dedicated approach to ongoing people development.

The result is probably best summed up by a former HP employee John Toppel, who now gives his time freely as an in-store sales consultant, who in an interview said, "I feel like I have two marriages; a wonderful marriage at home for 36 years and a wonderful marriage at HP. I guess that's now a former marriage, but I still have strong feelings for it".

Personal leadership review and learning

1. Do you have any long-term employees in your group or team? Are there people who have recently left the organization that it would have been beneficial to retain? Does your organisation have a mandatory retirement age? Does your organisation have a formal mentoring plan?

2. At a personal level, what are the leadership lessons you can draw from this and your personal experiences about working with older employees?

3. What can I (or my organization, my team) do differently (or keep doing) to make good use of older employees? For instance:
   - What should I do more of?
   - What should I do less of?
   - What should I keep doing?

4. Is there something I now need to plan for as a result of this learning? If so, what?

Team Learning Exercise

Use this story if you have older employees, or there is an opportunity to employ them.

1. Distribute the story prior to your meeting and ask everyone to read and answer the following questions (as usual, feel free to pick and choose the questions, or add your own):
   - What distinguishes an older employee from a younger one? (other than age) Why?
   - How should older employees be treated? Is this any different from others? Why/Why not?
   - How can we make the best use of our older employees?
   - What can you do at a personal level to maximize the benefits of older team members?
   - What support do you suggest your manager (and/or the organisation) provide to boost the role or use of older employees?

     WHAT TO DO WHEN **LEADERSHIP IS** NEEDED

2. At the meeting decide which questions if answered well, will be most beneficial to the team.

3. Lead a discussion on the selected questions to reach consensus on:
   - What action needs to be taken?
   - By whom?
   - By when?
   - How will our results be measured? When?

Author's note

I recently came across a firm that had two long term employees retiring. One had been there 41 years and the other 32! The firm, as part of the retirees celebrations, made a short video featuring them and thanking them for their loyal service. The video was posted on their website and social media.

Further suggested reading

New Zealand Work Research Institute, *Understanding the needs of New Zealand's ageing workforce,* https://workresearch.aut.ac.nz/ data/ assets/pdf_file/0005/378932/2015- Understanding-Ageing-Workforce-report,-FOW.pdf August 2015.

Erickson, T. *Leading from the Base of the Beanstalk,* Harvard Business Review, 21 May 2010.

Points to add to my Leadership Plan at the back of the book:

STORY 16:
15 JULY 2013

Can you really work from anywhere?

Productivity still counts as a metric that matters. With all that's been written about productivity, what counted most in the midst of the Covid pandemic? And if the claims of enormous productivity improvements aren't real, what is, and how can you create the conditions for productivity?

Chapter Objectives

- To help design work practices that provide productivity – but also include engagement, commitment, learning, growth, innovation and contributions to the organisation and community as a whole.

Chapter theme

With much hype about increased productivity of people working from home, are there any downsides? What type of workplace best suits your team/organisation?

Can you really work from anywhere?

Google's Chief Financial Officer, Patrick Pichette, ruffled a few feathers when he told the Sydney Morning Herald that he believed working from home is not the best way to generate ideas and innovation.

Pichette was visiting Google's Australian office and a local start up business community, when he made some unexpected comments on the topic of working from home (WFH).

"The surprising question we get is: 'How many people telecommute at Google?" Pichette said. "And our answer is: 'As few as possible'."

"It's somewhat counterintuitive. People think, 'Well, because you're at Google you can work from anywhere.' Yes, you can work from anywhere, but many just commute to offices... Working from the office is really important."

If you hadn't read the date at the start of this chapter, you'd be forgiven for thinking that Pichette was talking lockdown times during the Covid pandemic (2021). In fact, it was 2013!

However, Prichette makes an important point that is often overlooked in the debate on how productive WFH (or telecommuting) can be – the need in certain jobs, organisation cultures and with certain personality types - for social interaction.

Pichette said he believed that working from home could "isolate employees from other staff."

"There is something magical about sharing meals. There is something magical about spending the time together, about noodling on ideas, about asking at the computer 'What do you think of this?' These are magical moments that we think at Google are immensely important in the development of your company, of your own personal development and building much stronger communities."

Yet seemingly contrary to Prichette's views, the percentage of people who WFH is growing. In the US for example, in 2013 it was estimated to be around 10% of the workforce, and post the Covid pandemic, has risen to 1 in 4 Americans, or about 25%.

In the UK. the proportion of people working from home more than doubled in 2020 during the Covid-19 pandemic, though it remained a minority of overall workers across the UK. The Office for National Statistics (ONS) said about a quarter of people (25.9%) had worked at home at some point in the week before they responded to officials conducting its annual population survey. It said that this compared with 12.4% of workers in 2019.

However, some staff were more likely to work from home than others in a reflection of the uneven impact and experiences of the health emergency across the UK – with much higher concentrations of workers doing their jobs from home in London than elsewhere - the highest proportion of home workers were in affluent suburbs. Is this indicative of the type of work these people might be doing?

So is WFH a good thing – either for the employer or employee? How do organisations decide whether to provide WFH arrangements for their people? And if you're an employee who has the opportunity to participate in WFH, is it right for you?

There's been a raft of research on this topic from as far back as the mid 1970s. The general result of such studies is that WFH can be very productive for both the employer and the employee. But there are caveats.

One study (Bloom et al Jan 2013) of a Chinese company running a call centre showed that when two groups of employees were compared over a nine month period, (one traditional office bound and the other WFH), the WFH group were far more productive. In fact, they were 13% more productive.

However, the authors point out that, "the job of a call center employee is particularly suitable for telecommuting. It requires neither teamwork nor in-person face time. Quantity and quality of performance can be easily quantified and evaluated. The link between effort and performance is direct. These conditions also apply to a range of service jobs such as sales, IT support, and secretarial assistance".

"Team Leaders/Managers could generate a report from the database of the performance of the team members daily and easily detect problems in individual employees' performance," they added.

In the Chinese example, the results of the experiment were so successful (for the company), they decided to offer all their call centre employees the option of WFH or working in the office on a permanent basis (they'd all originally also been given the opportunity to volunteer for the WFH experiment).

Yet surprisingly, over half of all the employees soon changed their minds, indicating the extent of employee learning about their own suitability for working from home. In particular, two thirds of the control group decided to stay in the office, citing concerns over the loneliness of home working and lower rates of promotion.

In reverse, half of the WFH group changed their minds and returned to the office – typically those who had performed relatively poorly at home.

My own observations about the growth in WFH arrangements is that over recent years the emphasis has been on providing flexible working conditions to encourage a more motivated and stable workforce.

In search of this, have the actual job factors been overlooked? It's an equally important consideration. For instance, looking at professionals who WFH, an earlier 2007 study found that:

- Jobs that are completed in their entirety by the employee are far more motivating
- Greater feedback from the job itself is associated with more positive outcomes
- Greater feedback from the manager is associated with more positive outcomes
- 'Lower need to deal with others in the job' is associated with more positive outcomes.

And as Prichette's comments indicated earlier, it's important to have face-to-face interactions. In many offices, serendipity is important:

bumping into people, seeing people in the corridor, talking socially over coffee (and yes, gossiping) – these things are important for building organisational culture.

It's clear that most workers do want to see their colleagues in person periodically as well as retain work-from-home flexibility. A study of 3,000 UK-based remote workers conducted in March 2021 by intelligent learning platform HowNow showed that more than two-thirds (67%) felt disconnected from their colleagues, while half (49%) said this sense of disconnection was having a negative impact on how they viewed their job. A similar survey from job-site Indeed showed that 45% of US remote workers missed in-person meetings with their colleagues, with 46% missing those work-related side conversations that happen in the office.

Also, it's well known that quite a lot of the ways that we make decisions in organisations aren't made in meetings. They're made in the corridors.

If we now consider some of this evidence, perhaps there's more behind Mr Prichette's remarks than even he realises. These are important considerations for senior managers and HR managers when making decisions about offering WFH options.

And for employees, it would be useful to look at the type of work on offer and one's own personality and work preferences, before making a decision to WFH, no matter how appealing it may seem.

Personal leadership review and learning

1. What's been your experience with WFH? What's worked for you, what have you enjoyed most? What have you missed? On balance, what would be your preference – WFH, work in the office, or perhaps hybrid - a combination of the two?

2. At a personal level, what are the leadership lessons you can draw from this and your personal experiences about working from home?

   WHAT TO DO WHEN LEADERSHIP IS NEEDED

3. What can I (or my organisation, my team) do differently (or keep
    doing) to improve our working conditions for employees? For
    instance:
    * What should we do more of?
    * What should we do less of?
    * What should we keep doing?

    Note: keep in mind the need for productivity and also the
    need to include engagement, commitment, learning, growth,
    innovation and contributions to the organisation and
    community.

4. Is there something I now need to plan for as a result of this
    learning? If so, what?

Team Learning Exercise

It's quite probable that many of your team will have experienced
WFH. The meeting discussion should therefore be quite insightful.

1. Distribute the story prior to your meeting and ask everyone to
    read and answer the following questions (feel free to pick and
    choose the questions, or add your own):
    * What are the benefits of:
      » Working from home?
      » Working in the office?
      » A hybrid of the two?
    * What type of:
      » Job/Role would be better suited to WFH arrangements?
        Why?
      » Person would be better suited to WFH arrangements?
        Why?
    * If the organisation has a WFH policy, how can our team make
      best use of it?
    * If the organisation does not have a WFH policy, should it
      have one? If so, how could you influence the organisation to
      develop one?

2. Lead a discussion to reach consensus on:
    - What action needs to be taken?
    - By whom?
    - By when?
    - How will our results be measured? When?

Author's note

I wrote the following short article during lockdown in New Zealand in 2021.

What happens when we can't shake hands anymore?

What happens when we lose the handshake? During and post Covid-19, we've been asked to avoid touching other people (outside our bubble). That, and being almost fanatical about cleaning our hands and social distancing, have put us in the enviable position of probably having the best results in the world for tackling the Corona virus pandemic.

But there may be downsides that we're not yet fully aware of. Let me backtrack for a moment.

Back in the 1970's in Romania, there were many orphanages caring for deprived children. In general, they were adequately fed and clothed. However, they were starved of something else – physical touch. Studies showed that these children were half their expected height and weight for their age. They were also socially underdeveloped and unable to build meaningful relationships.

More recently in the US, and on the upside of non-touching, nurses working with premature babies have found that they develop faster when physically stimulated regularly.

Another series of studies compared pre-school children in Paris, where kids touched one another a lot, to those in Miami where there was less touching. Results showed that the French children were less aggressive both verbally and physically to others, than their US counterparts.

And there have been many other studies which show how important 'touch' is to our relationships, particularly how we feel about one another (both personal and in business).

     WHAT TO DO WHEN **LEADERSHIP** IS NEEDED

One of the most common ways touch is used is to communicate — and we do that through the handshake. At its most basic level, the handshake communicates trust, goodwill, or agreement with a common decision — for instance we often start and finish a conversation with others we are meeting, with a handshake as 'bookends' to our discussion.

So, what's happening to our important need for 'touch' as a result of Covid? It's suggested that we 'touch elbows' (not really touching), or perhaps more humourously, 'touch feet' (of course, whilst maintaining our social distance!). And then in business it's been meeting via Zoom, Google, Skype and so on, where there is no hope of touching.

And when talking with a friend recently about handshakes, she put another spin on it when she said "I think handshakes are really important to our culture as is the Hongi (a traditional Maori greeting in which people press their noses together) because they signify our preparedness to get along together".

I too am now a little worried that Covid may have some detrimental effects on our person-to-person relationships.

What's the answer?

I'm certainly not suggesting we break the rules and start handshaking again (during lockdown). But there are two things we can do.

Firstly, and here I need to return to the research for a moment, we need to hug people in our bubble more often, particularly at the start and end of the day, and when either or both are facing an imminent challenge. Why? The research has shown that hugging has a positive impact on our mental well-being by decreasing cortisol (the stress hormone) and increasing serotonin (antidepressant and anti-pain chemical). So, more hugging please! (in the bubble, of course!).

Secondly, try using more 'feeling' type words when meeting someone and when concluding the conversation. Feeling words whilst not replacing physical touch, often describe touch. For example, you might start with, "It's great to be able to meet face-to-face again and see one another in person — it feels really good". You could also conclude with something along the lines of "Great to meet up and touch base once again. Very much looking forward to the time we can really shake hands".

Further suggested reading

Harris, C. *Working from home is more complicated than we thought.* Stuff, Jan 17, 2021. https://www.stuff.co.nz/business/123891998/ working-from-home-is-more- complicated-than-we-thought

Consultancy.com.au, *Employee Engagement Has Fallen While Working From Home,* 18 July 2021 https://www.consultancy.com.au/news/3656/ employee-engagement-has- fallen-while-working-from-home

Points to add to my Leadership Plan at the back of the book:

STORY 17:
26 FEB 2008

Is business acumen a substitute for leadership?

At the top of organisations, which are more important – management skills or business skills?

Chapter Objectives

- To design strategies for developing managers in three skill areas:
  » Business skills (relevant to the industry)
  » Strategic planning skills
  » People management skills

Chapter theme

Many management development processes have focused on the development of people management and leadership skills to the exclusion of business (knowledge) and strategic planning skills. There needs to be a balance of all three, particularly at the higher levels of the organisation.

Is business acumen a substitute for leadership?

At the top of organisations, which are more important - management skills or business skills?

Take the case of hedge fund managers. Hedge fund managers are investment experts. They generally represent a small group of very wealthy people and organisations. They follow the financial markets in an endeavour to predict fluctuations and invest accordingly.

First set up as far back as 1949, hedge funds have four principal areas of investment. They short-sell stocks that they think will decrease in value; they use computer systems to calculate the relative value of one stock against another and then short the more expensive one and buy the cheaper – so-called "fair value". They also take on bankrupt or merging companies where a profit can be seen. Finally, they trade stocks by taking positions on the direction markets, currencies and commodities are likely to move.

As investment funds following these strategies, they had been extremely successful. That was until 2008. Their failure to manage financial risk, saw their performances plummet. In some cases they closed up shop altogether. For example, Sailfish Capital Partners, a $2 billion fund, closed in January 2008.

But even before the financial crisis brought on by the sub-prime failures in the US, some fund managers were having difficulty in another area. Many of those who moved away from their original investment strategies into taking a direct role in the management of the organisations they invested in, had run into trouble.

Is this a case of not 'sticking to the knitting', or a lack of business acumen?

Press reports of one such fund manager at the time, provides some clues. Edward Lampert, a hedge fund maestro, masterminded the takeover and merger of Sears and Kmart in 2005. Then he took on the role of Chairman of the new company. Now it seems that Lampert has found that actually managing an organisation is a bit different to investing in its stock.

Since gaining control of the organisation, Lampert as Chairman, took a very hands-on approach to management. And that approach had been based on his own expertise (finance), not the expertise of the business – retailing.

So, for example, the key underpinning of his strategy was to raise prices, cut capital spending and slash marketing budgets.

To head up the new organisation, he also appointed as CEO, Aylwin Lewis. Lewis was an expert in the fast food industry, not retail. However, despite appointing a new CEO, Lampert still maintained his hands-on approach to management.

The result?

Customer visits and sales went down, and so did profits. Those involved in face-to-face retail, know that people want an 'experience' when they shop. Sure they want the best price, but they also want to be treated as people (customers) first, not numbers on a balance sheet.

When shopping, often people buy based on their emotive response to the retail experience and then support their decision with reason and logic, such as price.

Yet Sears were obviously not providing this. As one newspaper report put it, "Stores ... look shabby next to those of rivals like Target and JC Penny. Dozens of products... were sold out. Much of the commodity merchandise that was in stock was more expensive than nearby competitors."

In other words, people are simply going elsewhere for their shopping experience.

The company has faced consistent quarters of decline since the merger of Sears and Kmart in 2005. For instance, income plunged 84 percent from 2005 to 2011. Eddie Lampert has remained as chairman over the period of decline, and according to industry analysts, feel the heart of the problem is his "penny-pinching" cost-savings by stifling investment into stores. Instead the company has been increasing its presence online. Is this the answer to declining sales?

On January 4, 2018, Sears Holdings announced it would close a further 103 unprofitable Kmart and Sears stores, after 24 quarters of sales declines. These stores would be closing by April 2018, leaving Sears with 555 stores. According to an op-ed in MSN money, "at this rate, Sears along with sister company Kmart, has an extremely high chance of disappearing and going defunct in 2018, and that 2017 will have marked its final holiday season as an independent brand". A tragedy for this once proud company that started business in 1886.

The message here?

People who run organisations such as active directors and CEOs, at the very least, need to be expert in the business of the business (non-executive directors are quite different and need to be defined by their business diversity, amongst other traits such as gender, age and ethnicity). This has been supported by two studies.

The first, PriceWaterhouseCoopers' annual CEO survey, found that organisations are first and foremost looking for senior executives with hard technical and business experience. People skills, whilst considered relevant, were not as high on their wish list.

However, one needs to be careful to read too much into this finding. For instance, are CEOs aware of the power generated by effective leadership and management or is it just getting harder to find experienced business people?

The second is a more robust study of actual behaviour of managers within organisations. The authors tracked over 1,000 managers at all organisational levels and found that in addition to cognitive and interpersonal skills, business skills and in particular strategic skills actually became more important as a manager progressed through the organisation.

So, if we are looking to develop managers to be business leaders, where should the balance be in management development initiatives – business or people skills?

My own observations over the last 30 years as a designer of management development processes, suggests that there has been a

     WHAT TO DO WHEN LEADERSHIP IS NEEDED

greater emphasis on people skills in training and development rather than pure business skills (I know my own efforts have often been in this direction).

This seems particularly true at the higher levels of management. Is it our expectation that managers at this level know all there is to know about business, but need to be made aware of the people power they can harness through effective leadership and management?

If we are to look at some of the business failures (particularly from the immediate post GFC era) and especially in the finance industry and compare these with the Mumford study findings, it would appear that there is an important lesson to learn.

Organisations need to look for both technical business expertise and good leadership skills when appointing senior managers. And that means that designers and providers of leadership and management development need to focus equally on the development of both strategic business skills and good leadership and management skills if they want their business offerings to be effective.

Personal leadership review and learning

1. What technical business skill development have you or your organisation carried out over the last 12 months? Similarly, what strategic planning has occurred?

2. At a personal level, what are the leadership lessons you can draw from this and your personal experiences about business and strategic planning development?

3. What can I (or my organisation, my team) do differently (or keep doing) to improve our business acumen and strategic planning skills? For instance:
   - What should I do more of?
   - What should I do less of?
   - What should I keep doing?

4. Is there something I now need to plan for as a result of this learning? If so, what?

Team Learning Exercise

This story may be useful as a pre-curser to the development of further business acumen in your people. It may also be useful as pre-reading for strategic planning sessions.

1. Distribute the story prior to your meeting and ask everyone to read and answer the following questions (as usual, feel free to pick and choose the questions, or add your own):

    - What additional technical business skills do we need to develop within the team? Why?
    - Do we have a strategic plan for the organisation? The team?
        a. How can we make best use of these?
        b. If we do not have either, how and when should we develop these?
    - How can we develop our business skills further? (suggest activities, training, exercises, etc.)

2. At the meeting decide which questions if answered well, will be most beneficial to the team.

3. Lead a discussion on the selected questions to reach consensus on:
    - What action needs to be taken?
    - By whom?
    - By when?
    - How will our results be measured? When?

Further suggested reading

Prince, E.T., *Business acumen: a critical concern of modern leadership development: Global trends accelerate the move away from traditional approaches.* Human Resource Management International Digest, https://www.emerald.com/insight/content/doi/10.1108/09670730810900811/full/html

Points to add to my Leadership Plan at the back of the book

MOTIVATING PEOPLE THROUGH PERFORMANCE MANAGEMENT

18. A NEW VARIETY OF CARROT?

- How to identify and develop the 'motivators' for effective team working

19. ARE YOU DEAD ON THE JOB?

- How to create a culture of recognition within the team

20. WHAT HAVE WE LEARNT ABOUT PERFORMANCE MANAGEMENT?

- How to manage and if needed, improve performance management processes

STORY 18:
22 MARCH 2012

A new variety of carrot?

When discussing motivation, the metaphor of the carrot and the stick appears to have been with us for a long time. Is there a new variety of carrot available to managers?

Chapter Objectives

- To identify the motivating factors present within the team and ensure they are maintained

- To identify factors within the team that may be inhibiting team members from producing their best work and eliminate or reduce them

- To develop strategies for developing effective teamwork

Chapter theme

Keeping team and group members both satisfied and motivated is a challenge for all managers. This chapter suggests some ways this may be achieved.

Is there a new variety of carrot?

When discussing motivation, the metaphor of the carrot and the stick appears to have been with us for a long time. It's been suggested that the carrot and stick approach was first used by peasant owners of donkeys in order to keep their animals moving. Whenever the animal stopped, the owner would dangle a raw carrot in front of the animal's nose (on the end of a stick). If the stubborn animal still refused to move, then guess what happened? The owner hit it with the stick!

Other suggestions for the origin of this metaphor purport that there was no punishment involved – the stick was merely used as a means of dangling the carrot at a reasonable distance in front of the donkey. So, the carrot was used purely as a 'motivator'.

Whatever the actual origins of the metaphor, news article headlines indicate that the metaphor of carrots as motivators is still alive and well, the following are examples of story headlines found in the press:

- *"The Right Carrot: Is Your Compensation Plan Keeping Your Sales Force Motivated?"*
- *"Dangle the Right Carrot to Entice Workers"*
- *"Offering the Right Sized Carrot"*
- *"Rewards and Praise: The Poisoned Carrot"*
- *"Sarkozy Referendum Pledge – A Carrot for Disgruntled Voters"*
- *"A $400 Million Carrot for Sears"*

Now, whether you adopt the carrot approach - getting people to do what you want them to do by rewarding them with something valuable they want, or punishing them if they fail to do what you want (perhaps reducing or taking away what is valuable to them) - it doesn't appear to work for all of the people all of the time. But can it work at all?

A report in the Tillamook Headlight Herald on Jun 27, 2012 posits an interesting point (Tillamook is a city in Oregon, USA that was trying to revitalise their downtown area), calling the carrot and stick approach 'affirmative maintenance'. Tillamook City Manager Paul Wyntergreen who previously managed the City of Jacksonville for 18 years, commented:

 WHAT TO DO WHEN **LEADERSHIP IS** NEEDED

"In Jacksonville we had an affirmative maintenance ordinance that would empower the City to clean up the property and place a lien on it, so that when the property was sold, the City was reimbursed," Wyntergreen said. "Tillamook doesn't have an affirmative maintenance ordinance. We have TURA (the Tillamook Urban Renewal Agency), which will partner with building owners and provide financial assistance in the form of grants and matching dollars.

"That is the carrot approach, to try to motivate owners to improve their property. An affirmative maintenance ordinance is a stick. Not that you want to use that stick; it's costly to the City. But combined with the carrot, it can be a means to leverage motivation."

Are these owners of neglected or rundown properties in Tillamook being 'motivated' by the affirmative maintenance scheme, or is there something else at play here?

Ever since the 1960s, theorists and academicians have considered the carrot/stick dichotomy a 'hygiene factor' in employee motivation, a term referencing Herzberg's two factor theory of motivation, published in his 1959 book, 'Motivation to Work'.

Readers will know that along with pay (more or less carrot and/or stick), Herzberg proposed the other two hygiene factors to be:
* working conditions, and
* supervision (i.e. fair and equitable management).

Herzberg believed that while the hygiene factors did not motivate people, taking them away or reducing them, greatly reduced an employee's satisfaction for work and ultimately their satisfaction with the organisation. He proposed that in addition to maintaining a sufficient level of hygiene for employees, there were other factors that needed to be in place to truly motivate them.

His 'motivating factors' (in today's terminology, the things that help deliver 'employee engagement') are:

- achievement,
- recognition for achievement,
- responsibility,
- meaningful interesting work, and
- the opportunity for growth and advancement.

Both the Motivators and Satisfiers are important, but for different reasons ...

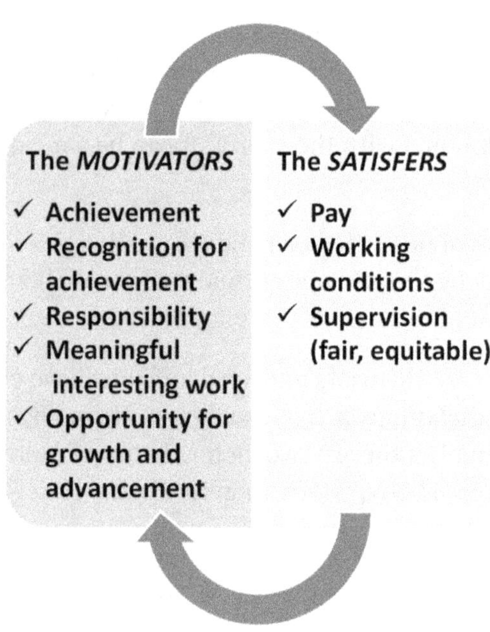

As a trainer and management educator, I've long been a strong proponent of Herzberg's model of motivation. However, at times I've struggled to convince hard-nosed business people that "money does not motivate people". After all, common sense suggests that if you offer someone something that is valuable to them, they're likely to do it for you. Reduce or take away this incentive and they are less likely to perform for you. That's the 'common sense' theory.

A study by the Kenexa High Performance Institute, which surveyed more than 31,000 workers from 28 countries about workplace issues such as managerial and leadership effectiveness, senior

   WHAT TO DO WHEN LEADERSHIP IS NEEDED

management behaviour, diversity practices, turnover intentions and job satisfaction, has thrown up some exciting evidence that seems to support both Herzberg's theory and the good common sense theory that we all see as 'valid'.

The study shows that for production, warehouse or clerical workers making less than $40,000 a year (remember, this was 2012), pay is positively related to employee engagement and their intention to stay with the organisation. Whilst the study shows this relationship is modest, it is indeed significant.

However, as income rises for professional, technical workers and management, the relationship diminishes. In other words, pay matters more to those making less, and for those in management no relationship between pay and employee engagement exists.

If you thought that result was interesting, here's the real kicker. Whilst for production, warehouse and clerical workers:

- *income* and *intention* to stay are modestly related,
- a belief in *opportunities for career advancement* is highly related to deciding to stay with an organisation.

So it would seem that whether in management, professional, clerical or production jobs, if people can see a future for themselves at the organisation, they are more likely to stay. These findings really help to clarify Herzberg's original model and show how we as managers can use this in a practical way to keep people both satisfied and motivated.

But the Kenexa study adds an important caveat to the original model:

> "According to the two-factor theory, hygiene factors do not add to motivation, they can only negatively affect satisfaction if they do not reach a certain threshold. In the case of line workers' income, it is likely that this threshold is the point at which the individual is living comfortably. Higher paid employees may set the threshold at a higher cost of living, or perceptions of fairness as they compare themselves to their peers.

Regardless of income level, after income reaches this threshold, it can only serve as a de-motivator; if income is taken away or perceived as unfair, employees will tip the scale by underperforming which manifests in behaviours such as not meeting goals, taking more sick days or leaving the job."

For some, these findings may not be surprising. However, as the report points out:

"Consider the amount of money spent on retention and performance bonuses, golden parachutes and salary increases for the very group who consider money as noticeably less relevant when deciding to leave a job. Granted, individual circumstances may vary, but in general, offering larger raises and bonuses to higher income groups is unlikely to raise this group's retention rates."

As a two-factor motivation supporter, I've often wondered why employer/employee negotiations are always based around pay, working conditions and supervision. Why don't the workers ask for more of the motivators? This report now helps me understand why.

What's the message for managers and organisations from these findings?

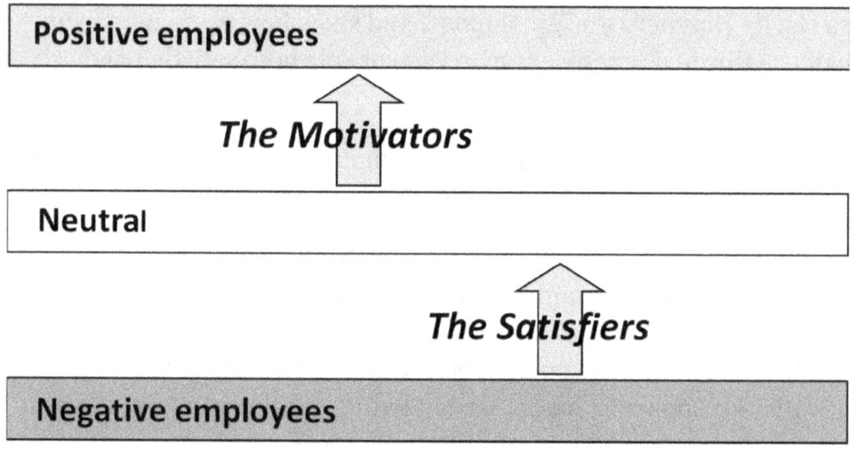

   WHAT TO DO WHEN LEADERSHIP IS NEEDED

Perhaps as we always have, we need to still focus on ensuring both the motivators and satisfiers are maintained and indeed enhanced.

Now there's a new challenge.

How do we package reward, recognition and remuneration so that it meets the needs of people at all levels of the organisation? This is indeed an exciting challenge.

We may need a new variety of carrot!

Personal leadership review and learning

1. What can we learn about motivation from this story?

    - As a Manager, what should I be doing TODAY to:

• Develop a real sense of ACHIEVEMENT in my people?	
• Increase the amount and quality of RECOGNITION I give people for their achievements?	
• Increase the amount and degree of RESPONSIBILITY people are given?	
• Develop people's work or role so that it is more MEANINGFUL and INTERESTING for them?	
• Increase people's opportunity for GROWTH and ADVANCEMENT?	

2. At a personal level, what are the leadership lessons I can draw from this and other stories about motivation?

3. What can I (or my organisation, my team) do differently (or keep doing) to encourage motivation within the workforce? For instance:

    - What should I do more of?
    - What should I do less of?
    - What should I keep doing?

4. Is there something I now need to plan for as a result of this learning? If so, what?

Author's note

'Motivation' is a topic that has fascinated people for centuries and what 'motivates' his or her people is one of a manager's ongoing challenges. What seems to work for one team member may not work (or not work so well) for another. Yet, as this story shows, there are some general principles that a manager can use to provide the best opportunity for all his or her employees to be the best they can be. Your challenge as a manager is twofold:

1. To engender within your work group or team, the general conditions that will enable all your people to perform at their best.

2. To identify specific 'motivators' that apply best to each of your individual team members.

Having used the following exercises many times with various types of work teams, I am constantly amazed at the discussion around 'What motivates people?' and the innovative ways managers and their teams apply some of the motivating factors. You may want to allocate at least half a day for the full exercise (or more if you wish to turn it into an Action Planning one) or break it up into two separate sessions.

Team Learning Exercises

This story can be a good starting point for discussing motivation. For example, people will often say they are motivated by money – and that's true, up to a point. Over and above that point, what else comes into play?

     WHAT TO DO WHEN LEADERSHIP IS NEEDED

There are two exercises for this story – you may choose to use either or both (separate sessions are probably a good idea if using both). Make sure to distribute a copy of this chapter to all your people before using either or both of the following exercises – this will enhance the meeting discussion considerably.

Team Learning Exercise #1 'Motivators and Satisfiers'

Part A: Individual exercise to be completed by all team members prior to a team meeting

1. Think of a time when you felt highly motivated:

    - What were you doing? Please list these examples (short descriptions will do) on a plain sheet of paper.

    - What made you feel so good at this time?

    - Why are these things so important to you?

2. Review your stories you've just listed in Step 1. Next, scan the article 'A new variety of carrot?' again for the description of 'Motivators' (you'll find there are five, starting with 'achievement'). From your stories, list the 'motivators' that were evident in your stories and give an example of each:

The MOTIVATORS	Examples of these in my stories...

Were any of the 'Satisfiers' evident in your story? Review the chapter again – you'll see there are three, the first being 'pay' (or money). If so, please list these below:

The SATISFIERS	Examples of these in my stories...

Part B: At the Team Meeting

1. Appoint someone as the meeting leader. Record key points on whiteboard or flip chart as they are discussed.

2. As a group, take it in turn to discuss your 'motivating' stories. List key 'motivating factors'.

3. Did anyone have any 'satisfiers' in their story? List these.

4. As a team, decide how best to:
   - Ensure the 'satisfiers' are maintained.
   - The 'motivators' are encouraged.

Team Learning Exercise #2 'Forces at Work'

Part A: Individual Exercise: To be completed prior to a team meeting or silently in the first five minutes of the team meeting.

Instructions

The matrix of Forces at Work on the following page lists 20 approaches to organisation in the workplace. These items are either facilitators or inhibitors.

Facilitators are those forces that enable and encourage people to perform to as high a level at work as they possibly can.

Inhibitors may be said to be the opposite. They tend to restrict people's ability to perform to their maximum potential.

There are 10 facilitating forces and 10 inhibiting forces in the matrix.

 WHAT TO DO WHEN **LEADERSHIP** IS NEEDED

The activity on the following page asks you to identify the 10 facilitating forces and the 10 inhibiting forces. This is an individual exercise, please complete it privately. You will then be asked to reach consensus with your fellow team members.

Forces at Work – The Matrix

1 Clear-cut goals exist at all levels: corporate, departmental and personal	2 Tight, well thought out job description for each individual member of the organisation	3 Freedom to fail	4 High corporate and personal performance standards
5 Opportunities for personal experimentation for all employees	6 Competitive system for promotion among peers	7 Strong, decisive, self-asserting leadership	8 Confident planning, directing and controlling by managers
9 Precedents for decision-making throughout the organisation	10 Involvement of individuals in the making of decisions which affect them at all levels	11 Close supervision and attention to task details	12 Staff critiques of their manager's performance

13 Tight organisational structure with clear-cut lines of authority	14 Openness and candour in manager-staff relationships	15 Emergent leadership based on situational demands and expertise of personnel	16 Conformity to established procedures and precedents
17 Group or team management practices	18 Strong budgetary controls on management and staff	19 Minimal pressures from immediate superiors	20 Challenging interpersonal and inter-departmental rivalries

The Task:

Your task is to identify the 10 facilitators and the 10 inhibitors. Please place your choices in the following table:

	#	#	#	#	#	#	#	#	#	#
Facilitators										
Inhibitors										

Part B: At the Team Meeting

1. Just prior to the team meeting, print out the matrix on a large sheet (A3 is ideal) and place on a flipchart stand. If this is not possible, draw up a rectangle of 20 squares on a flipchart or whiteboard, listing each square from 1 to 20 (no need to write out the full description in each square, it's easier to use a shortened version such as "1. Clear cut goals").

2. If the total team is say, more than seven members, split the team into two smaller groups. When the team is more than seven, splitting them into two groups will provide a much

 WHAT TO DO WHEN **LEADERSHIP IS NEEDED**

richer discussion (it can also provide some competition between the two smaller groups).

3. Ask the people in the team (or each smaller group) to share their answers with one another by listing 'F' or 'I' on the flipchart 20-squares. So, for example if there are five members in the group, then they might list their answers on the flipchart for question 1 as "F, F, I, F, I". List everyone's answers to all 20 items before commencing any discussion – this way the group can see immediately where there is agreement or disagreement (coloured pens for each member can be useful to identify who answered "F" or "I" to each of the 20 items).

4. The aim of the team (or smaller groups) is to reach consensus on which of the 20 items are:
    - Facilitators - those forces that enable and encourage people to perform to as high a level at work as they possibly can.
    - Inhibitors – those forces that tend to restrict people's ability to perform to their maximum potential.
    Note: Groups should strive for consensus, not majority vote. Consensus means that everyone's view should be heard and discussed, so that the group is comfortable with their final group answer. For example, Question 1, although starting out as "F, F, I, F, I" may, through discussion, end up with a group answer of "I".

5. Once the team (or smaller groups) have reached consensus on all 20 items (remember there are only 10 'F' and 10 'I' items, so they may have to go back and discuss one or two items until they have only 10 'F' and 10 'I' squares), share the 'official' results. Then lead a discussion on agreement or disagreement with the official answers, and why.

6. Following agreement, ask the team to identify:
    - Those items from the 10 Facilitators that are in place in our team and working well.
    - Those Facilitators that are missing from our team – what can the team do to ensure the missing Facilitators are initiated, developed and encouraged?

- Those items from the 10 Inhibitors that are present in our team (or perhaps the organisation). What can we do to eliminate or lessen the negative impact of the Inhibitors?

"Official" Results

Note here the use of the word "Official", that way any dissenting members/teams can argue with me (the author) rather than the meeting facilitator. Good luck!

	#	#	#	#	#	#	#	#	#	#
Facilitators	1	2	3	4	5	10	12	14	15	19
Inhibitors	6	7	8	9	11	13	16	17	18	20

Note; The results of the discussion regarding which Facilitators and Inhibitors are present in our workplace, can be the start of an excellent planning session to ensure the Motivators and Satisfiers (discussed earlier) are being well embedded in the workplace culture.

Further suggested reading

Herzberg's Motivators and Hygiene Factors: Learn How to Motivate Your Team, Mind Tools, https://www.mindtools.com/pages/article/herzberg-motivators-hygiene- factors.htm

Points to add to my Leadership Plan at the back of the book:

STORY 19:
22 MAY 2018

Are you dead on the job?

Our greatest reward is receiving acknowledgment that we have contributed to making something meaningful happen. More than anything else, people want to be valued for a job well done by those they hold in high regard.

Chapter Objectives

- To develop a culture of recognition within the team.

Chapter theme

Praise, the thing that makes us all feel good, is often overlooked in the corporate environment – and yet unlike pay, it costs nothing – it's free!

Are you dead on the job?

There's a story doing the rounds about the worker who was dead at his desk for three days before anyone discovered him. The press report purportedly read:

> "Bosses of a publishing firm are trying to work out why no one noticed that one of their employees had been sitting dead at his desk for three days before anyone asked if he was feeling okay.
>
> George Turklebaum, 51, who had been employed as a proof-reader at a New York firm for 30 years, had a heart attack in the open-plan office he shared with 23 other workers. He quietly passed away on Wednesday, but nobody noticed until Saturday morning when an office cleaner asked why he was still working during the weekend.
>
> His boss Elliot Wachiaski said: 'George was always the first guy in each morning and the last to leave at night, so no one found it unusual that he was in the same position all that time and didn't say anything. He was always absorbed in his work and kept much to himself.'
>
> A post mortem examination revealed that he had been dead for three days after suffering a coronary. Ironically, George was proofreading manuscripts of medical textbooks when he died."

True or not, there is an important message in this yarn. Have you been appreciated at work lately? Whilst pondering this question, keep in mind that appreciation is a two way street - we also need to appreciate the work of others.

We all want to be associated with a winner, be it a winning person, a winning team, a worthwhile cause or a successful organisation. We all have sports people, teams, actors or artists that we consider "ours".

When they do well, we bask in their reflected glory. It's the same at work - we want to be associated with a worthwhile, winning organisation. Our greatest reward is receiving acknowledgment that

   WHAT TO DO WHEN LEADERSHIP IS NEEDED

we have contributed to making something meaningful happen.

More than anything else, people want to be valued for a job well done by those they hold in high regard.

A famous study by Lawrence Lindahl in the 1940's came up with some surprising results when supervisors and their employees were asked to list "What motivates employees?"

Employees listed "appreciation of a job well done" as number one and "feeling in on things" as number two.

Supervisors, on the other hand, expected the employees would rank these two items as eighth and tenth respectively (supervisors thought employees would put "wages" as number one and "promotion" number two).

These results have been replicated time and time again ever since. In another recent study, employees were asked to rank job-based incentives. "Personal thank-you's" came first and "a note of appreciation from my manager" came second. "Money" came in at 16th!

Praise, the thing that motivates us the most, takes so little time and costs nothing. Famous management writer Rosabeth Moss Kantor once said "Compensation is a right. Recognition is a gift."

Have you appreciated the work of others lately? Has the value of your own work been appreciated? Here's a quick test:

Over the last week, have you done any of the following?
- ✓ Told someone they have done a good job?
- ✓ Looked specifically to find someone doing something well?
- ✓ Made someone else look good rather than taking the credit yourself?
- ✓ Thanked others for your own success?
- ✓ Passed on positive comments you have heard about others?

These are simple examples of the things we need to do regularly to acknowledge the good work of others.

You might say, "If it's that easy, why don't more people do it?" There are many reasons, but they all fall into two categories - personal and organisational.

On a personal level, many of us are not comfortable giving praise. We may be awkward about it, or perhaps believe that people are paid to do a job, so why do we have to praise them?

From an organisational perspective, it may be the culture that is holding us back, or perhaps technology preventing us from valuing the work of others. For example, technology has changed the way many of us operate. Email, text, Zoom and even working from home, may have replaced personal interaction, so we no longer see what others do well. Out of sight is out of mind, so how can we praise good work if we don't see it?

Here are six ways we can put praise for a job well done back into our working lives:

1. Look for things people do well and acknowledge them for their good work.
2. Be a model of acknowledgement - show others it's OK to give praise.
3. Have a conversation with a colleague about how to give praise for work well done.
4. When people have performed above the norm, write them a small thank you note (not email or text).
5. Encourage others to thank one another and pass on stories of others' good work to your manager.
6. Work to create a culture of appreciation - make acknowledgment part of your daily routine.

Finally, to get the ball rolling, pass this chapter on to a colleague as an introduction on how you both can encourage others to give more praise.

The essential point is that praise must be frequent and given locally (by colleagues and managers). It should not be seen as a corporate initiative or program, but merely 'the way we do things around here'.

What's not been said so far, is that praise must be genuine. People in general are very good at spotting insincerity.

The message?

When you do praise someone, make sure it's for the good work they have done and not just for the sake of it.

A final word of warning. Many organisations turn acknowledgement into an event. They distort it with extrinsic motivators (such as money) and taint it with internal competition. Pure and simple, giving praise for a job well done is just that - pure and simple.

So, find someone doing something good today and simply tell them what a good job they've done. Above all, tap people on the shoulder occasionally to make sure they are still alive!

Personal leadership review and learning

1. What are the messages in this story? Why is 'appreciation for a job well done', so often overlooked, or even considered unnecessary?

2. At a personal level, what are the leadership lessons you can draw from this and your personal experiences about giving praise and recognition?

3. What can I and my team do differently (or keep doing) to improve the culture of recognition both locally and in the wider organisation? For instance:
   - What should I do more of?
   - What should I do less of?
   - What should I keep doing?

4. Is there something I now need to plan for as a result of this learning? If so, what?

Team Learning Exercise

This story is a useful pre-curser to a team discussion on 'recognition'.

1. Distribute the story prior to your meeting and ask everyone to read and answer the following questions (as usual, feel free to pick and choose the questions, or add your own):
    - Why is 'giving praise' so important to people?
    - Think of two or three occasions when you were praised for a job well done. What was said? By whom? How did it make you feel?
    - How can we develop a culture of recognition within the team? (suggest activities, events, meetings, training, exercises, etc. plus personal things that everyone should do on a daily basis)

2. At the meeting decide which questions if answered well, will be most beneficial to the team.

3. Lead a discussion on the selected questions to reach consensus on:
    - What action needs to be taken?
    - By whom?
    - By when?
    - How will our results be measured? When?

Further suggested reading

The following has excellent examples that have real meaning of how to give recognition to people – well worth the four minutes it takes to read. Enjoy!

Cadieux, M., *3 Easy Steps to Give Powerful Employee Recognition,* Applauz Blog,
https://www.applauz.me/resources/how-to-give-employee-recognition

Points to add to my Leadership Plan at the back of the book:

STORY 20: 15 FEB 2010

What have we learnt about performance management?

As Performance Management Systems are now part and parcel of most organisations, they at least need to be designed in such a way that they encourage managers to 'manage' rather than allow managers to rely on some bureaucratic system as a crutch for poor management.

Chapter Objectives

- To highlight the need for regular performance management discussions.

- To identify the skills required to participate in an effective performance review discussion (both team member and manager).

- To list ways the team can improve performance reviews using the existing performance management system.

Chapter theme

Should performance management be a backward-looking review of results, or is there a better way to encourage employees to perform at their best?

What have we learnt about performance management?

What did management learn from the global economic crisis (in 2008) about getting the best out of their people? Two examples of the way in which people's performance is managed, suggest that the answer might be "a lot" and "not much".

In the first case, it was reported that auto maker GM, the recipient of large government handouts following the GFC, had actually improved its performance management system. Under the old system, senior managers were evaluated quarterly on criteria that were spelt out in exhaustive detail. Such reviews were many pages long – in fact they needed to be contained in a ring binder!

As Terry Woychowski, former GM Director of Engineering said at the time: "We measured ourselves ten ways from Sunday." It was in fact a performance measurement system, not a performance management system.

In their new performance management system (PMS), GM managers are evaluated using simpler criteria. The performance review is contained on a single page. It is annual, and they are held accountable for previously agreed performance goals.

Then there's the case of the troubled A.I.G., another recipient of government funding following the GFC. What did they learn? How were they going to improve their management processes?

Under the headline of "A.I.G. Roles Out New Pay Plan" (New York Times 10 Feb 2010), a brave new performance based pay plan was announced. Under their new scheme, people's performance will be graded numerically which will be tied directly to their performance bonus.

Robert H. Benmosche, A.I.G.'s chief executive was the brainchild behind the scheme. Perhaps bowing to extensive public pressure to reduce the enormous bonuses paid to employees (or at least to be able to justify them at the time of the GFC), he was reported to be introducing a forced ranking system for employees' performance.

As the NY Times article reported: "Under the new system, employees will be ranked on a scale from 1 to 4. Those ranked number 1, a group expected to be no larger than 10 percent, will receive much more in annual bonus payments, according to an A.I.G. spokeswoman. Those ranked 2 or 3 — together comprising about 70 percent of A.I.G. employees — will be considered as having performed above or in line with expectations. Those ranked 4 will receive lower incentive pay."

Sound familiar? Yes, it's almost the same as the 20-70-10 scheme previously used by G.E. where employees were ranked A, B or C on the basis that there should normally be 20% above expectations, 70% meeting expectations and 10% below expectations – commonly referred to as 'the normal distribution curve'.

The difference apparently with the new AIG scheme, is that those ranked 4 (or C in the G.E. model) will not be immediately pushed to leave the firm as they were at G.E. (known colloquially as the 'rank and yank' scheme).

Will this new 'incentive based scheme' be effective? Time will tell. However, if the G.E. experience is anything to go by the answer could be problematic. Some people suggest that the GE 'yank and rank' scheme was responsible for a 28-fold increase in earnings and a five-fold increase in revenue between 1981 and 2001 (that was also the year that Jack Welch left G.E.).

Critics of such schemes however, label them as a 'competitive' model of managing performance (people compete against one another to achieve a better ranking) as opposed to cooperative. Even the statisticians have got onto the critique bandwagon by showing that over time, assuming that the intended aim of the scheme is successful (to get people to improve their performance and thus their ranking), there will be more As and Bs and less Cs. But is this really what happens?

When managers are forced to rate their employees, say from 1 to 4, or A, B, or C, personal factors come into play - like favourites and personalities - and managers and employees spend more time networking and carrying favour to highlight their accomplishments

     WHAT TO DO WHEN LEADERSHIP IS NEEDED

than actually achieving them. But the unhealthiest result, experts say, is the fact that someone on the work team will be pigeonholed as a failure. So for example, if a manager has a work team of 10 which is achieving great results and every one of those ten is performing at their best, how can two or three, be rated as 'failing'?

Even President Barack Obama had something to say on the AIG scheme at the time: "It's hard to understand how derivative traders at AIG warrant any bonuses, much less $165 million in extra pay. How do they justify this outrage to the taxpayers who are keeping the company afloat? In the last six months, AIG has received substantial sums from the U.S. Treasury. I've asked Secretary Geithner to use that leverage and pursue every legal avenue to block these bonuses and make the American taxpayers whole. This isn't just a matter of dollars and cents. It's about our fundamental values.

All across the country, there are people who work hard and meet their responsibilities every day, without the benefit of government bailouts or multi-million dollar bonuses. And all they ask is that everyone, from Main Street to Wall Street to Washington, play by the same rules."

If readers' comments on the NY Times article are anything to go by, the AIG system may have been doomed before it started. Here's a taste of how some readers responded:

- *Employees will be ranked by whom, based on what? Unless the "what" is directly tied to long term profitability there will be no curbs on risk taking for short term profit. If employees ranked 3 are described as "having performed... in line with expectations," then by definition those ranked 4 will have not met expectations. Yet, "those ranked 4 will receive lower incentive pay..." means that even if they do not meet expectations, they will receive incentive pay (a.k.a. bonus).*

- *What it fails to do is link incentives with risk containment — not an easy task, but necessary to avoid future financial crises.*

- *So essentially nothing changes at A.I.G. Your bonus is now openly based on how much you suck up to your manager, not on any real measure of competency (though "competency" and "A.I.G." is an oxymoron at best).*

There were no positive comments for the new A.I.G. scheme. So, what's been learnt here? It appears that in the GM example, emphasis is placed on 'managing' performance. The new Chairman of GM suggested the changes were part of a much needed cultural change throughout the organisation, where layers of bureaucracy are being cut and wider managerial responsibilities are being given to a younger cadre of managers. "Replacing a binder full of job expectations with a one-page set of goals is just one sign of the fresh start."

On the other hand, one gathers that at A.I.G. the emphasis will be on measuring performance after the event rather than proactively managing performance as GM are doing.

Can you imagine yourself sitting down to do a performance review in either GM or A.I.G. either as a manager or receiving the review? I'm sure your mindset would be quite different in both cases. I've long been a critic of performance management systems, particularly those linked to individual pay incentives – nothing should take the place of good management.

However, as they are now part and parcel of most organisations they at least need to be designed in such a way that they encourage managers to 'manage' rather than allow them to rely on some bureaucratic system as a crutch for poor management. Whilst the economic crisis might have been the catalyst, it's generally agreed that poor management got both organisations into real trouble. The way they manage their people had to change.

From their pre-crisis performances, both companies seemed to be in need of cultural change. It will be interesting to observe the results of the two quite different change processes over the coming years.

Author's note

There are at least two points to make about this story – one concerning AIG and its performance since introducing its new PMS; the second about the simplicity of the new GM one-page performance management system.

Firstly AIG: It can take years, if not decades, to wash off the residue of propping up private companies with public funds. It should be noted that when the $182.3 billion the US Treasury loaned AIG through the Federal Reserve Bank of New York was paid back (June 2015) it generated a $22.7 billion profit for the government via its sale of AIG shares (AIG also sold off several businesses to repay the loan).

That said, even a relatively happy ending to government intervention seemed to be overshadowed by a simple public relations gaffe; when AIG paid back its initial round of bailout money, company pride called for a series of YouTube videos about AIG's honesty and forthrightness. When the reaction to these videos turned overwhelmingly negative, AIG decided to disable comments. Was it a 'simple public relations gaffe'? What does this 'gaffe' say about the 'new' culture at AIG? Interesting that AIG disabled negative comments from the public.

Secondly, the one-page GM performance management system – do such systems work? Studies have shown that overall, traditional performance management systems improve employee performance in about one third of cases, have little or no impact in another third, and have a negative impact on performance in the remaining third of cases. So, organisations need to be very careful with the type of PMS introduced.

There's only anecdotal evidence to support this so far, however, one-page forward looking, performance management (often called 'feedforward' rather than 'feedback') is seen to be far more effective than backward oriented 'appraisals'. As one manager commented, "My regular performance discussion with team members focuses on three questions: How are you doing? How am I doing? How can I help?"

Personal leadership review and learning

1. Having read this story, what impact do you consider your organisation's PMS has on individual and team performance?

2. At a personal level:
    - What are the performance management lessons you can draw from this and your experiences with performance management (both as a manger and a team member)?
    - If a colleague were to ask you about your own performance management of your team members, what would you say? Why?
    - If you were to develop a new one-page PMS, what would it contain? How often would you use it? What impact do you believe it could have on your team members?

3. What can I (or my organization, my team) do differently (or keep doing) to help develop better performance management? For instance:
    - What should I do more of?
    - What should I do less of?
    - What should I keep doing?

4. Is there something I now need to plan for as a result of this learning? If so, what?

Team Learning Exercise:

This team exercise should be run as a 'workshop' where team members work individually, in pairs and as a total team, to develop a more positive approach to managing performance. It is not intended to change the existing PMS, and the outcomes of this meeting should be complimentary to your existing PMS. It has three components:

Activity #1: Expectations for a successful performance review (PR)
Activity #2: Experience and learnings from previous PRs
Activity #3: Skills required for participating in a successful PR

Step 1: Ask team members to read this chapter prior to the team meeting.

Step 2: At the meeting, split team into pairs (Activity #1). Time in pairs for Activity #1 should be a total of six minutes. Give the following worksheet to each team member and ask people to interview one another – they have three minutes per interview.

<table>
<tr><td colspan="2">Workshop Activity No. 1 – Expectations for a successful performance review</td></tr>
<tr><td colspan="2">Please spend 3 minutes interviewing the person next to you. (They should then reverse the role). Work quickly, six minutes maximum for this exercise.</td></tr>
<tr><td>1. Person's name:</td><td></td></tr>
<tr><td>2. Approximately, how many Performance Review sessions (or appraisals) have you been involved in? (This and other organisations)</td><td></td></tr>
<tr><td>3. What do you consider to be the major concern(s) people have about these sessions?</td><td></td></tr>
<tr><td>4. What would you like to learn more about when participating in PR sessions?</td><td></td></tr>
<tr><td>5. What do you think would be a successful outcome from today's team workshop on performance reviews?</td><td></td></tr>
</table>

Step 3: Conduct a discussion around answers to questions 3, 4, and 5 (above):

- Concerns people have with performance reviews.
- Things people would like to see covered in a performance review.
- Successful outcomes expected from today's team meeting.

Step 4: Ask team members to spend three minutes completing the following questions in Activity #2. They should then discuss their experiences with their partner for a further 5 minutes.

<table>
<tr><td colspan="2">Workshop Activity No. 2 – Experience and learnings from previous PRs</td></tr>
<tr><td colspan="2">Think back to a previous appraisal or performance review interview you have had (this could be either a 'good' or 'bad' session). Please list:</td></tr>
<tr><td>What did the other person do and say that made the session either effective or ineffective?</td><td>What did you do or say that helped make the session either effective or ineffective?</td></tr>
<tr><td></td><td></td></tr>
</table>

Step 5: Following this discussion in pairs, **ask team members to spend a further three minutes completing the following questions in Activity** #3. They should then discuss their experiences with their partner for 5 minutes.

<table>
<tr><td colspan="2">Workshop Activity No. 3 – Skills required for participating in a PR</td></tr>
<tr><td colspan="2">Discuss with your colleagues. Please list:</td></tr>
<tr><td>The skills required by the person conducting the PR session to ensure that it is effective are:</td><td>The skills required by the employee whose performance is being reviewed are:</td></tr>
<tr><td></td><td></td></tr>
</table>

Step 6: Conduct a discussion around answers to:
- Things the other person said or did in the PR. Why were they effective/ineffective?
- Things you said or did. Why? What were the results?
- The skills required for both a manager and team member to participate in an effective performance review.

Step 7: Conclude team meeting with a discussion on:
- What can we do to improve the performance reviews conducted in conjunction with our existing PMS?

 WHAT TO DO WHEN LEADERSHIP IS NEEDED

- What does each team member need to do . . .
    - » Prior to the discussion with the manager?
    - » During the performance review session with the manager?
- What does the manager need to do . . .
    - » more of
    - » less of
    - » keep doing

    to ensure performance reviews are as successful as they can be?

Further suggested reading:

Zenger, J. The 6 Vital Elements Of Effective Performance Management Systems, Forbes Feb 16, 2017 https://www.forbes.com/sites/jackzenger/2017/02/16/the-6-vital- elements-of-effective-performance-management-systems/?sh=311553fb618e

Points to add to my Leadership Plan at the back of the book:

LEADING YOUR PEOPLE TO PROVIDE GREAT CUSTOMER SERVICE

21. DO YOU KNOW WHO ARE YOUR CUSTOMERS?

- How to distinguish between consumers and customers

22. SERVICE WITH A SMILE

- How to develop a customer service orientation within the team

STORY 21:
21 APRIL 2008

Do you know who your customers are?

Knowing who your customers are is the foundation for any successful organisation. And as the US Federal Aviation Administration demonstrated in April 2008, getting this wrong can be disastrous..

Chapter Objectives

* To distinguish between 'customer' and 'consumer'.

* To identify who are our customers.

Chapter theme

Identifying who the real 'customer' is and distinguishing between 'customers', 'consumers', 'clients' and 'suppliers' is essential for business success.

Who is your customer?

To any savvy business manager, that may seem a simple or even silly question. "Of course I know who my customers are, I wouldn't be in business otherwise" might be the natural response.

But one organisation that got this drastically (and what could have been tragically) wrong - and which almost crippled an entire country (well at least for a couple of weeks in 2008) - was the US Federal Aviation Administration.

The US Transportation and Infrastructure Committee held House hearings in April 2008 into the airline industry. Jim Oberstar, former chairman of the committee, said its investigation uncovered a pattern of regulatory abuse and widespread regulatory lapses, allowing 117 aircraft to be operated commercially although not in compliance with FAA safety rules. Oberstar said there was a "culture of coziness" between senior FAA officials and the airlines and "a systematic breakdown" in the FAA's culture that resulted in "malfeasance, bordering on corruption".

And as CNN reported on one such example at the time:

> Southwest Airlines tried to keep serious problems with its maintenance program hidden and pressured the Federal Aviation Administration to keep out an inspector who noticed the problems, according to two FAA inspectors who blew the whistle on the airline.

> Bobby Boutris and Douglas Peters told CNN Wednesday they brought information about Southwest's lack of compliance with mandatory inspection protocols to their supervisors, but the FAA did nothing. Boutris said the airline tried to have him removed from the inspections.

> "My supervisor called me into his office ... and told me he had had a meeting with the director of quality assurance and the AD [airworthiness directive] compliance leader from Southwest Airlines, and he had requested my removal from the inspection," Boutris said.

As the New York Times commented in an opinion piece 'Fear and flying and the pathetic FAA':

> When a federal agency refers to the industry it oversees as its 'customers' a boundary has been dangerously crossed. As representative James Oberstar, the chairman of the House Transportation and Infrastructure Committee rightly said last week, "The FAA's only customer is the air-travelling public."

These press reports highlight two important issues. The reporter was right when saying "a boundary has been dangerously crossed". James Oberstar was wrong when saying "The FAA's only customer is the air-travelling public."

Before looking further at the FAA and its 'boundary' and 'customer' issues, let's start at the beginning. As any experienced Organisation Development person will say, getting the answer to "Who is my customer?" correct, is the foundation stone for any successful business.

Take two common examples to illustrate.

In the first, the manufacturers of popular brand-name soap powders such as Persil (which by the way has been around since 1903 – now, that's success!), have clearly identified you and I as their customer.

We are also the consumer.

Although they sell to shops and chain stores, all their marketing is aimed at getting you and I, their customers, to select their product when we enter the store, not someone else's. And although they sell the soap to the shops, the stores are distribution channels, not customers. When you and I (the customer of the soap manufacturers) like their soap and buy more of it, the shops stock more of that brand. So, we are both customers and consumers.

The second case is the manufacturer of high quality furniture. Unlike soap powder where most people (well, at least those who do their own washing) can name three or four brands, you and I would be hard pressed to name one brand of high quality furniture.

In the case of high quality furniture, we are still the consumer, but we are not the manufacturer's customer. The furniture store is their customer. The manufacturer's sole aim is to market to the high-end retail stores to stock their furniture and not someone else's. Until we see and feel the furniture (and possibly not even then) do we know what brand we are about to consume.

How does the correct identification of 'customers' relate to the FAA's problems?

Here's an example to illustrate. In a similar way to the FAA, in the 1980s the Australian Taxation Office was faced with mounting criticism over the service it was providing to the tax-paying public. After much soul searching (and probably the services of a good OD consultant), they decided their only customer was the Treasury (the government).

But they still had their poor service image to fix. Cleverly, they decided to call the tax paying public their 'clients'. The critical point here was that they kept clearly in mind that the one and only true customer they had, whose needs, expectations and requirements must be met at all times, was the Treasury.

If the FAA had identified that the US Government (through the appropriate Senate Committee) was their one and only customer, they would not have been in the situation they were in, in April 2008. They would have been focusing on the safety standards required by their customer (the US government), not trying to appease the airlines.

How did this confusion for the FAA come about?

When the airline industry was deregulated in 1978, someone within the FAA, decided that they needed to give better service to the people they dealt with most regularly, namely the airlines. And that service should be 'customer service'. So, by default, airlines became the FAA's 'customers'.

Now we all know that 'customers are always right', Right? When an organisation starts to think erroneously of a key stakeholder as their customer, their entire mode of operation changes. No longer do they meet the needs, expectations and requirements of their real customer (because they haven't identified who that is).

As airline passengers, you and I are customers. Not of the FAA, but of the airlines. The FAA has only one customer – the US government. It is the FAA's sole responsibility to ensure that it is meeting all of its customer's very high standards, one of which is 'safety'.

As customers of the airlines and consumers of the product, you and I put our faith in the fact that the airlines have been regulated by an organisation that is at all times meeting its customer's needs, expectations and requirements.

And that's why it is so important to be clear about how any business handles the perennial statement, 'the customer is always right'. First, one has to know, 'Who is the customer?' Right!

Personal leadership review and learning

1. The principles underpinning successful organisations are clear in this story:
   - What are these principles?
   - Does your organisation have a clear idea of who their customers are?
   - Are your customers and consumers the same group? Is this important to identify for the success of your organisation?
   - Who are the customers of your team? Is your team aware of this?
   - Who are your suppliers? How are they managed?

2. At a personal level, what are the service lessons you can draw from this and other stories about customers, consumers, clients and suppliers? Why are these nomenclatures so important?

3. What can I (or my organization, my team) do differently (or keep doing) to ensure we are clear on who our customers are? For instance:
   - What should I do more of?
   - What should I do less of?
   - What should I keep doing?

4. Is there something I now need to plan for as a result of this learning? If so, what?

Team Learning Exercise

This story is a useful pre-curser to a team discussion on 'customer service'.

1. Distribute the story prior to your meeting and ask everyone to read and answer the following questions (feel free to pick and choose the questions, or add your own):
    - Thinking about the whole organisation, who is our customer? (Note: there may be more than one group)
    - Who are our team's customers?
    - Are our 'customers' also 'consumers' of our service / products? Does this make a difference to the service we provide? Why/Why not?
    - What do our team's customers expect from us? How do we know?

2. At the meeting decide which questions if answered well, will be most beneficial to the team.

3. Lead a discussion on the selected questions to reach consensus on:
    - What action needs to be taken?
    - By whom?
    - By when?
    - How will our results be measured? When?

Further suggested reading

No suggested readings for this chapter. If you come across a good one, please let me know.

Points to add to my Leadership Plan at the back of the book

STORY 22: 1 JUNE 2018

Service with a smile

Until managers can work out what motivates people, their efforts at improving customer service will have no greater impact than what has been tried before. There's no substitute for good management and authentic leadership when engendering excellent customer service within the organisation or team.

Chapter Objectives

- To determine how our team can provide the best customer service possible.

- To develop both a team and individual 'To Do' list to achieve our ideal customer satisfaction team.

Chapter theme

Distinguishing between 'products' and 'services' in customer satisfaction is critical. Is this achieved through providing staff with extrinsic motivators, or is there something more simple, yet little understood?

Service with a smile

"Products are consumed, services are experienced" Harvard Business School Professor Theodore Levitt, is reported to have said.

I had the pleasure of seeing this distinction in action. Some years ago, my wife had employed a new manager for her team. To take the job, the new manager had to relocate (with her husband) from Melbourne to Sydney. As the couple were new to Sydney, we took them out to dinner at our local favourite restaurant.

The evening went extremely well with as usual, both the food and service first class. Then when the desserts arrived, piped in chocolate around the outside of our guests' plates were the words "Welcome to Sydney". Obviously our waitress had listened and taken note of the early conversation we had with our guests, informed the chef, and the result? One of the most memorable service experiences I have encountered (my wife's manager, still talks about that 'fabulous dinner' many years later).

As we all know, getting front line staff to provide excellent, even good customer service, seems to be the perennial management challenge. This appears even more challenging when times are tough and businesses are scrambling for that extra sale.

So how do organisations meet this challenge? Following are three examples.

The first is an old one that had been tried before and was trotted out once again in the US by Delta Airlines. In 2008 they revived their 'Red Coats' customer support service (dropped in 2005 when Delta was in Chapter 11 bankruptcy).

For those in the US old enough to remember, the 'Red Coats' scheme was probably named after the US railway's 'Red Caps' – the porters who provided excellent service to rail passengers (they're still around in some places, but who travels by rail anymore?).

The idea behind the Red Coats service is that these people are out with the customers answering questions and helping out, rather

   WHAT TO DO WHEN LEADERSHIP IS NEEDED

than behind the counter. And the Delta Red Coats are able to issue boarding passes from hand-held machines. All in all, they don't have any more responsibility than their counter-staff colleagues, but they are paid more!

Along similar lines and around the same time, American Airlines gave bonuses of $100 to $200 to customer service representatives who met certain service satisfaction goals (could this be 'tipping' by another name?).

However, a different approach was tried in Japan. Tokyo railway workers at Keihin Express Railway Co. have the option of checking the degree of their smile on a 'smile meter'. Using a digital camera on top of their PCs, customer service staff are able to get a reading on how well they are smiling before they start their service shift.

The smiling rating goes from "0" (grim faced) to "100" (a very broad smile). Company managers (who can also test their smiles) believe that "a smile goes a long way" to providing excellent service (anyone who has travelled on the Tokyo subway can attest to the service challenges these staff face, and the service they provide in very challenging circumstances).

By now you can no doubt spot the different management philosophies at play in these three approaches. The first, Delta is changing some team member's mode of operating and paying them more. The second, American Airlines, are bribing people to perform. In both cases these staff are not being given any more responsibility than others. The third example, at Keihin Express Railway Co, which is optional, leaves it to the individual (both managers and service staff) to take direct responsibility for their own performance.

Which approach to service will be most successful?

Well, if history can be any gauge, US airlines have been notoriously poor performers in the area of customer service. For instance, in the airline survey by Skytrax in 2009, there were 34 airlines in the world rated higher than Delta or American – both of whom, only got a 3-star ranking. By comparison the six 5-star service airlines were all

Asian, as were 12 of the 29 4-star airlines. By 2017, Delta was at No. 32 (up from 35 in 2016), and American Airlines came in at No. 74 world-wide.

What underpins these results? Consider the difference in managing service performance between Asian and US airlines - and the lack of ratings improvement in the two US airlines. As any well-read student of customer service will tell you, service starts with management. If managers treat their staff the way they want their staff to treat the customer, then they will get good service results. Should Delta and American managers be rewarded for treating their staff better? Would this make any difference?

Now, you could say that there are cultural issues that impact the differing results here (Asia and the US). And you'd be right. But there is also a very important management principle in play that seems to have been overlooked by the US airlines – what really motivates people to perform at their best?

You might think that I am being rather hard on the US airlines. Well, those Asian airlines who have tried the 'bribery' approach have also failed. One such attempt was tried by Garuda with fatal (yes, cost of human life) results. In March 2007, an Indonesian Garuda Airlines Boeing 737 crashed on landing at Yogyakarta airport in Java. 21 people died and scores were injured - a deadly toll when you pay people to perform (as you'll see shortly). Press reports at the time suggested that the crash might have been caused by the pilot trying to save fuel by going ahead with the landing rather than making another attempt.

"A Garuda policy of preserving fuel may have been why a pilot did not abort a landing in Yogyakarta last month that killed 21 people", the head of the Indonesian airline pilot's association said. He added that he was concerned about Garuda's policy of paying pilots a three per cent bonus if they conserved fuel. "The company is making extra payments to pilots if they can conserve fuel. Maybe this is bothering the pilots."

Not only is this a disturbing safety concern, it raises the contentious issue of individual pay for performance.

  WHAT TO DO WHEN LEADERSHIP IS NEEDED

So, what really motivates people to perform at their best and provide excellent service?

Until the US airline managers and others with similar mindsets, can work out what motivates people, their efforts at improving customer service will have no greater impact than what has been tried before. There's no substitute for good management and authentic leadership – and do they understand Levitt's distinction that "Products are consumed, services are experienced"?

Personal leadership review and learning

1. What went well or not so well in these stories?
    - There are four stories here – two positive and two not so positive. From your reading, what's working in the two positive stories that is not evident in the others?
    - What should all organisations avoid if they want their people to provide good service?

2. At a personal level, what are the leadership lessons you can draw from these and other stories about customer service?

3. What should I (or my organisation, my team) do differently in the delivery of the service we provide to our customers?
    - On a scale of 1 to 10 (10 being the highest), how would you rate the service currently provided by your people?
    - If this rating were to improve, what would both you and your team need to do?

4. Is there something I now need to plan for as a result of this learning? If so, what?

Team Learning Exercise:

This chapter is a useful pre-curser to a team workshop on customer service. Distribute a copy of this chapter together with the following pre-work to your team:

Pre-work Item

Our "Ideal" Customer Satisfaction Team
(Insert your team's name and organisation name here)

Assume that it is now (insert a date 12 months from the date of the workshop). Our team has been working productively together for the last 12 months. Teamwork is good. We have also had many compliments from our external customers as well as others within the organisation about the good service we provide. Write down your answers to the following three questions:

1. What did we do to achieve such good results? (both as individuals and as a team)

2. What challenges or problems did we have to overcome?

3. What did we do to meet these challenges and overcome these problems?

At the workshop

1. Run a discussion around the four stories in this chapter:
    - What were the good points?
    - What were the things we should avoid?
    - What's the distinction between 'products' and 'services'? How does this distinction apply to us?

2. Ask team members to propose descriptions of our 'Ideal Customer Satisfaction' team (Pre-work Question 1). Remember; it is now 12 months into the future and we are looking back on our good results over the last 12 months. Summarise their responses.

3. Ask team members to contribute answers from their pre-work on:
    - What did we do over the last 12 months to achieve such good results?
    - What challenges or problems did we have to overcome to achieve these good results (Pre-work Question 2)?
    - How did we overcome these challenges (Pre-work Question 3)?

4. Lead a discussion to reach consensus on:
    - What action needs to be taken to reach our 'ideal'? What do we:
        » need to do more of?
        » need to do less of?
        » keep doing?
    - By whom?
    - By when?
    - How will our results be measured? Who will know? When? What will others say?

5. Finally, ask each team member to complete an individual 'TO DO' List (see below). Make sure you also complete one. You may care to conclude the session by revealing some of your 'TO DO's'.

My Potential 'TO DO' List

I will now implement the following activities in my day-to-day work:

Action I am taking	I will know I am successful because ...

Author's Note

In this workshop, it will be easy for people to say things such as "Oh, we can't do that because ...". Keep reminding people that we are now 12 months ahead in time and we are looking back on the last 12 months, so there are no impediments or barriers to the actions we have taken, merely the challenges we have overcome during the last 12 months.

It is a good idea to write the date (12 months in the future) prominently on a flipchart or whiteboard and mention it a few times to let people know about where and when they are (you could even make a few 'back to the future' comments or references).

This is not ignoring current limitations the team may face. These can be 'parked' if they continue to come up, on a flip chart or whiteboard. You can then address these towards the end of the workshop. In this way, people will most likely have proposed suggestions on how to address current impediments by the time you get to discuss the 'parked' items. Even if this has not happened, the team will undoubtedly be now looking at overcoming them in a more positive and constructive manner.

Further suggested reading

Hyken, S. *The Cult of the Customer: Create an Amazing Customer Experience that Turns Satisfied Customers into Customer,* Sound Wisdom 2020.

Levitt, T. *What business are you in? Classic advice from Theodore Levitt,* Harvard Business Review https://hbr.org/2006/10/what-business-are-you-in-classic-advice-from-theodore-levitt

Points to add to my Leadership Plan at the back of the book

DEVELOPING *CREATIVITY* WITHIN YOUR PEOPLE

23. WHAT'S WORKING AROUND HERE?

- How to initiate ways of developing the best products and services

STORY 23:
29 MAY 2018

What's working around here?

Over recent years there has been an increasing body of research that can help point us in the right direction to help develop innovation and creativity.

Chapter Objectives

- To identify ways that the team and all members of the team can contribute to improving how we deliver quality services and products.

Chapter theme

The ability to develop creativity within a team, rests on three foundation stones:

- establishing a culture where the intrinsic motivators are valued;
- providing structured processes that free people up to exhibit their innovative talents; and
- an organisational culture that encourages people to 'speak their mind'.

What's working around here?

There was a nice story in the press (Dallas Morning News March 2, 2008) about a 78 year old scrap metal worker, N.L. Jones. Given the opportunity to apply his creative talents to scrap metal and wood by his employer John Hargrove, over two decades Jones turned this useless material into thousands of bird houses. And in the process, created a new product and market for his employer.

"I wouldn't be in business if it wasn't for Mr. Jones," said Hargrove, who bought the salvage operation 20 years ago. Other employees left after the sale, but "Jones probably felt sorry for me and stayed. He showed me where everything was. Told me what everything cost. What to buy and not buy."

N.L. Jones was a man willing to give, who would donate his birdhouses to charitable causes and support his employer when times were tough. "He'd say, 'I won't cash my check. Things will get better,'" Hargrove said.

When the economy is tight, or in a downturn, it highlights the need for managers to foster such creativity and innovation. But how to do it?

Thankfully, over recent years there has been an increasing body of research that can help point us in the right direction to develop innovation and creativity.

Not surprisingly, 'intrinsic motivators' our old favourites, come to the fore in the research. For example a study of hotel workers in Hong Kong found that the risk-taking dimension necessary for creativity was correlated to the intrinsic job-related motivators. These include:

- Opportunity for advancement and development
- Loyalty to employees
- Appreciation and praise of work done
- Feelings of being involved
- Sympathetic help with personal problems
- Interesting work

If these sound familiar, you're right – they are almost word for word the same as the intrinsic job motivators put forward by Frederick Herzberg more than half a century earlier.

Historically, hospitality was simply concerned with providing accommodation and food for travellers. Emphasis was placed on the operational routine work of how hotels satisfy travellers for accommodation and food needs. However, this research indicated that creative ideas put forward by staff, generated business benefits to the hotel.

As with all employee development, and particularly that related to 'creativity', the genesis rests with the manager. It goes without saying, that if you expect employees to be innovative, then it must start with the manager.

This was confirmed in a major study published in the Academy of Management Journal, where it was found that managers could assist the development of innovation within their employees by:

- Providing high levels of autonomy
- Encouraging people to use a wide variety of skills
- Enabling people to identify with the job
- Ensuring the job had sufficient significance within the organisation

     WHAT TO DO WHEN LEADERSHIP IS NEEDED

- Providing personal feedback and ensuring the job had built-in feedback

By comparing the two lists from these two studies (employees and managers), it's clear how much congruency there is. If managers provide the 'right' conditions, employees are more likely to be creative in their work.

So, the intrinsic motivators are the foundation stones. To build the creativity edifice, one more thing is needed – a creativity schema – a process that encourages people to think differently and make creative contributions.

Many will be familiar with one of the best creativity processes, the Six Thinking Hats concept (the creation of Edward de Bono). This process can be used individually, in creative brainstorming or even normal team meetings to foster the creation, development and implementation of new ideas, concepts and products. As with all of de Bono's ideas, it's simple yet highly effective.

In short, de Bono's Six Thinking Hats is a structured process to assist teams to be more creative, realistic and practical in their decision making. During a meeting, the team works through a process of 'wearing' each of the six hats as they move towards a decision or plan.

Here's a description of de Bono's six hats ...

Green Hat	White Hat	Black Hat
• Ask – What other alternatives are there? • Modify existing ideas • Provide new insights / directions • How would this work in the next century?	• Talk and think logic, data and information • Assess relevance of information • Assess accuracy of information • Separate fact from fiction	• Name the possible and existing negatives • Exercise caution • Make judgment and assessment of an issue or decision

Red Hat	Yellow Hat	Blue Hat
• Identify feelings and emotions • Name gut reactions • Anticipate how others might feel about this issue or decision	• Encourage positive aspects of thinking and look for positive words • Express the benefits • Accept all suggestions / thoughts, even if they seem way-out or not feasible	• Manage the thinking process and the conversation progress • Get the best out of everyone • Focus and refocus, thinking • Keep an overview of what's happening

In overview . . .

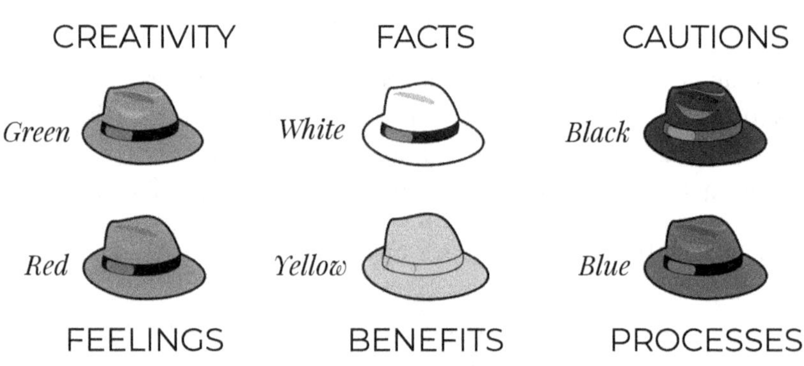

Creative processes such as Six Thinking Hats, can be used on an ongoing basis too. For example, where the team has used the Six Thinking Hats process in previous meetings, during a subsequent meeting the manager might say "Let's put our Green Hats on for a moment and see how we might develop a range of options on this issue". Or, when a particular team member is appearing to be overly negative on an issue, the manager might say, "John, I wonder if I could ask you to take your Black Hat off for a moment. Try a White Hat approach for a few moments. If this were to work, what would be the logic behind it?"

 WHAT TO DO WHEN LEADERSHIP IS NEEDED

Another creative process that also works well is the establishment of 'Art Shows' where individuals and teams display their latest improvements on coloured posters which are posted on walls. These posters not only include improvements made in work practices, products etc, but also communication processes such as project management, change management and negotiation.

One company that introduced the 'Art Show' concept (they called it a "Day in the Sun") set up these posters in the cafeteria one afternoon each month. All employees were invited to visit the cafeteria, view the exhibits, have a coffee and talk with the individuals and teams who had posted their ideas. The ensuing development of improved ways of working across the organisation was quite amazing.

We've talked about the intrinsic motivators as being the foundation stones for developing creativity within team members, and the manager's 'creative schema' (team processes) which build the creativity edifice. But over and above encouraging the intrinsic motivators, helping managers develop their 'creativity schema' by using creativity processes, there's the essential requirement of a positive corporate culture – the ground where teams need to work together and build.

If the organisation as a whole is to foster innovation and creativity, the key influencers in the organisation must demonstrate a positive mind set. Unfortunately, as managers we quite often look to 'fix problems' rather than encourage innovation. In a study by Ipsos Public Affairs (2007), 88 percent of US workers considered themselves to be creative. But when it came to creativity in the workplace, just 63 percent said their positions were creative, and a comparable 61 percent thought similarly about the companies for which they work.

So for example, when developing corporate culture, one can readily see the difference in attitude that quickly occurs when two different types of questions are posed to employees. If managers ask say, five or six employees; "What needs to be fixed?", they will be presented with a list of complaints which in fact are often minor but start a negative discussion. Over time, such negative discussions lead to negative cultures.

On the other hand, when managers ask this same group of employees "What's working around here?", they'll start a meaningful discussion about some of the key drivers that make the organisation successful, and ultimately lead to the development of a positive corporate culture.

Some organisations have used the 'What's working around here?' approach by bringing groups of people from across the organisation together for short sessions. In these sessions, participants discuss in pairs their answers to "What's working around here?". The facilitator then draws out many of their answers and the group decides on three key drivers that the organisation will focus on over the coming months. This process is simple, inexpensive and encourages the development of innovation and creativity.

As a manager in these challenging times, will your team be throwing out the unusable scrap, or building new bird houses? You may well ask, "What's working around here?"

Personal leadership review and learning

1. Do you need to have your people think more creatively? What have you done to encourage their creativity?

2. At a personal level, what are the leadership lessons you can draw from this and your personal experiences about developing creativity and innovation?

3. What can I (or my organisation, my team) do differently (or keep doing) to develop a culture of innovation and creativity within the team? For instance:
    *   What should I do more of?
    *   What should I do less of?
    *   What should I keep doing?

4. Is there something I now need to plan for as a result of this learning? If so, what?

Team Learning Exercise

This chapter can awaken team members to the need for innovation. Conduct a team meeting along the following lines:

1. Have team members read this chapter.

2. At the start of the meeting, ask team members to answer the question "What's working around here?" with at least six answers. Allow five minutes for team members to individually develop six answers.

3. Split team into pairs. Each pair is to share their list of six items, then decide on three (only) that are the best three that describe "What's working around here?"

4. Have pairs share with the main team, their chosen three items.

5. Lead a discussion with the aim of finalising the 'three best things that are working well in our team'.

6. Conclude with a discussion on:
   - What should we do more of?
   - What should we do less of?
   - What should we keep doing?

7. You may wish to include the results in an action plan with responsibilities and dates.

Further suggested reading:

De Bono, E. *Six Thinking Hats,* Little Brown and Company, 1985.

Points to add to my Leadership Plan at the back of the book:

COMMUNICATING TO INFLUENCE

24. ARE YOU A VIRAL MANAGER?

- How to understand the emotional impact of our communication

25. HOW GOOD ARE YOUR LISTENING SKILLS?

- How to improve our ability to listen for the real messages

STORY 24:
12 JUNE 2018

Are you a viral manager?

There are at least two elements to consider when endeavouring to influence others — firstly the content and the way the topic is presented (the intent), and secondly the emotional impact it has on the audience. Often managers miss the opportunity to impact their audience by not considering the potential 'emotional' component of their message.

Chapter Objectives

- To consider the emotional impact our communication has on the intended audience.

- To design and develop more effective messages and communication strategies.

Chapter theme

Fostering change is about changing people's perceptions. Most often, we try to change others' perceptions by explaining the reasons and logic for the change. Decades of research in social psychology have shown that people often share strong emotions as a means of fostering connection and solidarity. It's a manager's ability to evoke these emotions within the intended audience that leads to changing mindsets, not the reason and logic behind the message.

Are you a viral manager?

The biggest thing to hit the news in June 2012 was 'Invisible Children – Koney 2012', a 30-minute video by the Invisible Children organisation aimed at garnering support against African warlords.

Why was this video so 'big'?

It went viral. In less than five days it had more than 70 million views (at last count it was over 100 million). This is a story about the abduction, mistreatment and ultimate radical indoctrination of children into a waring way of life. So why did it go viral? And why this video when other organisations have produced similar topic videos (including Invisible Children) without such social media success in the past?

Does a video have to have a certain topic content to go viral? Do these viral videos have to have anything in common?

For example, 'Britain's Got Talent' 2009 runner-up Susan Boyle whose song 'I Dreamed a Dream' got me smiling (and crying) again when I watched it as research for this chapter (it had over 70 million views within six days). Or Rebecca Black, the 13-year-old who made a funky song video 'Friday' into one of the most popular and (depending on your viewpoint), disliked videos of 2011. Then there are the animated videos of less than 30 seconds that have hit the big time.

And for sheer outright career success, my favourite has to be 'United Breaks Guitars' that turned little known Canadian country singer Dave Carroll into an overnight success. The song was penned by Carroll as a result of the lack of service and compassion he experienced when his Taylor's Guitar was broken by United Airline baggage handlers. By October 2017, the YouTube video had received 17.7 million views (as I write this chapter in 2022, it's now over 21 million views!). Taylor now travels the world as a public speaker on organisation culture and its impact on customer service.

So, what makes something go viral, and what relevance does this have to management, and particularly a manager's ability to influence others?

The jury is still out on the answer to the first part of this question ('going viral', although I feel, getting very close to a verdict). However, there are some very interesting theories that may go some way to explaining this phenomenon. In so doing, there may also be some thought provoking messages for managers - perhaps in the way we communicate and in particular, the way we successfully influence and engender change in the workplace.

There are at least two elements in the answer to this question – firstly the content and the way it's presented (the intent), and secondly the emotional impact it has on the audience.

According to YouTube's Trends Manager Kevin Allocca and other experts on the subject, there are a number of essentials for a video to go viral:

1. There should be at least one or more 'tastemakers' (e.g. Oprah Winfrey) that promote the video. Then the community (local or global) participates and becomes part of the video (e.g. in 'Invisible Children' you are asked to sign a pledge before viewing – you feel as though you have contributed to the making of the video).

2. The unexpectedness of the video or characters that behave in a way that is totally shocking, surprising or comical for the occasion (e.g. Susan Boyle, a 47-year-old somewhat overweight woman from a small Scottish village with some might say, limited visual appeal or professional presence who surprisingly possessed the most wonderful singing voice. Her video now has over 21 million views on YouTube).

3. Community participation – 'community' here meaning a cohort group (e.g. in the case of 'Invisible Children' over 90% of the initial viewers were under 25).

4. The message is compelling and heart touching.

Are you starting to see a nexus between viral videos and the way managers successfully stimulate change in the workplace?

The first three are classic change management principles, i.e.:

1. Find the biggest supporters or blockers of change and get them involved in the change process.

2. Show people the unexpected. For example take something from the old that is important to them and something they thought would be shelved or completely done away with, and make it a key part of the new.

3. And of course, involve people in the change process itself (planning, execution and follow-up). In particular, look for cohort groups – find their particular needs and work with them to satisfy these needs.

It's the fourth element that I find managers overlook most – making the change a compelling and heart touching event or process. After all, it's not management-like to talk of feelings – the soft stuff. It's much easier to explain the change in terms of logic and reason, which we then find to our dismay, doesn't always have the impact we intended.

Research supports the need we all have for a compelling and heartfelt message. According to a study by Jonah Berger, Assistant Professor of Marketing at the University of Pennsylvania's Wharton School, it has to do with the visceral emotions it arouses in viewers. When people are physiologically aroused, whether due to emotional stimuli or otherwise, the autonomic nervous system is activated. This then boosts social transmission. Simply put, evoking certain emotions can help increase the chance a message is shared.

How important a lesson for the messages managers must communicate is this new evidence!

If people are sharing messages, it shows a real interest in the content. As Berger reported, "In a prior paper, we found that emotion plays a big role in which New York Times articles make the most emailed list. But interestingly, we found that while articles evoking more positive emotions were generally more viral, some negative emotions like anxiety and anger actually increased transmission while others like sadness decreased it. In trying to understand why, it seemed like 'arousal' might be a key factor".

This led Berger to his current study. In the study, Berger suggests that feeling fearful, angry, or amused drives people to share news and information. These types of emotions are characterised by high arousal and action, as opposed to emotions like sadness or contentment, which although also emotional, are characterized by low arousal or inaction. "If something makes you angry as opposed to sad, for example, you're more likely to share it with your family and friends because you're fired up," Berger contends.

Why does this desire exist? Decades of research in social psychology have shown that people often share strong emotions as a means of fostering connection and solidarity. "If I'm angry, and then you get angry, we can bond over what we're feeling" Berger says.

The internet does not usually provide the opportunity to share these emotions in normal Facebook, tweet, text, email messages etc. (although there are mixed results in the study of whether emoticons elicit emotions in the receiver – generally, other factors such as word choice come into play). It's only when a video clip or news article embodies all the viral elements and particularly the compelling and heart touching one, that people share these messages and in the process, their feelings.

There is one part of Berger's study that is particularly relevant for managers. Subjects who were aroused emotionally were found to be far more inclined to email even a neutral online article to friends than those who were unaroused. As Berger points out, the implications of this study are quite broad. "People's behaviour is heavily influenced by what others say and do. Whether you are a company trying to get people to talk more about your brand, or a public health organization trying to get people to spread your healthy eating message, these results provide insight into how to design more effective messages and communication strategies."

So as a manager, if you're looking to foster connections between people, solidarity, empowerment or change, then keep in mind that your message must not only be sound and logical but must also touch the heartstrings of your people.

Are you a viral manager?

Author's note

This chapter contains a number of short examples of viral messages
rather than a story. On this basis, it is probably more relevant to
individual managers in their endeavours of change management
rather than teams, unless your team is set up as an agent of change,
such as introducing a new system, product or service. The following
questions are therefore directed towards managers to reflect on
and inspire their change management initiatives. However, I've also
included a team exercise for change agent teams.

Personal leadership review and learning

1. What have been the results of your change initiatives? Was there
    acceptance or push-back? Why?

2. At a personal level, what are the leadership lessons you can draw
    from this and your personal experiences about initiating change?

3. What can I (or my organisation, my team) do differently (or
    keep doing) to ensure our change initiatives are accepted and
    successful. For instance:
    - What should I do more of?
    - What should I do less of?
    - What should I keep doing?

4. Is there something I now need to plan for as a result of this
    learning? If so, what?

Team Learning Exercise

Quite often problem-solving meetings or change meetings don't
reach their full potential because the meeting dwells too much on the
present or past situation, rather than 'how things ought to be'.

Providing the problem, issue or initiative has been clearly defined,
the following design will ensure that your change management
meetings are productive:

1. Every participant should be asked to prepare for the meeting at
    least one week in advance.

     WHAT TO DO WHEN LEADERSHIP IS NEEDED

2. The meeting pre-work should consist of a one-page answer to the 'Meeting pre-work question'.

3. The 'Meeting pre-work question' must be framed on the assumption that the problem has already been solved, or the change has already occurred – i.e.. it must be expressed as some future time. For example, if a call centre service department were looking for ideas on how they might improve their service, the question might be put:

   "Assume that we have just had a very successful year, and that we have received heaps of feedback which suggested our service given to customers has been first rate over the last twelve months:
   - *What things did we do to get such great success?*
   - *What problems or challenges did we have?*
   - *How did we solve these problems or meet these challenges?"*

4. At the meeting all participants' ideas should be extracted and listed on flipchart paper. The team should then reach consensus on which are the most important items to address.

5. When the meeting has reached consensus on which items are worthwhile and achievable, two further columns are added to each flip chart page. One column is headed 'By when' and the other is headed 'By whom'.

6. It is important that the workload is shared by all participants. In the first column 'By when', the group is asked to allocate a time for when this aspect could be achieved. When this is agreed, people are asked to volunteer to undertake responsibility for ensuring particular items are undertaken (not necessarily to do them), by placing their name in the 'By whom' column. The meeting now has an action plan for solving the problem or undertaking the change.

Further suggested reading
(in this case, viewing and listening)

Carroll, D. United Breaks Guitars, https://www.youtube.com/watch?v=5YGc4zOqozo Carroll, D. United Breaks Guitars 4. Dave Carroll Responds to Customer Service incident on United Flight 3411 https://www.youtube.com/watch?v=yQz8qqioCt8

Boyle, S. I Dreamed A Dream, https://www.youtube.com/watch?v=yE1Lxw5ZyXk

Points to add to my Leadership Plan at the back of the book

STORY 25:
15 MAY 2015

How good are your listening skills?

Listening skills enable a manager to understand intentions and feelings of their team, an essential skill for team management. Your employees will be more open, positive and motivated if they feel they are being heard and will strive to do their best for the team if they feel they and their ideas are being heard.

Chapter Objectives

- To improve the quality of our listening.

Chapter theme

Much of management communication training is on how to speak positively and with authority – important qualities. Just as important is the other side of the coin which is less seldom taught – listening. The following short chapter and learning exercises are aimed to correct this imbalance.

How good are your listening skills?

How good are your listening skills? Really good? Enough to bet your life on? Because that's what British woman, Ingrid Loyau-Kennett, did in May 2015 when she calmly confronted two men who had just slashed another man to death in a busy London street.

At the time a passer-by's phone video showed one of the suspects excitedly facing the camera, covered in blood and still holding a knife in his hands. He'd just killed off-duty soldier, Lee Rigby.

As Loyau-Kennett's bus turned a corner, out of her window on the right-hand side of the lower deck she saw a body lying in the middle of the road and a few feet away, a car smashed into a lamp post on the pavement. Her "gut instinct" moved her to jump off the bus to offer first-aid assistance for what she believed to be a road traffic accident.

But a few moments later she was being confronted by two men holding a selection of butcher's knives and a gun in their blood-drenched hands.

As one press report described the scene, "She is slight, dressed in jeans and a navy body warmer, with her hands tucked into her pockets. A daffodil is pinned to her top buttonhole. The attacker, his eyes dark with anger, towers over her. Blood is spattered on the sleeves of his black coat, drops sliding off the knife he clutches in his left hand."

Speaking later about the incident, Loyau-Kennett said, "And then when I went up there was this guy with a revolver and a kitchen knife, he had what looked like butcher's tools and he had a little axe, to cut the bones, and two large knives and he said 'move off the body".

"So I thought 'OK, I don't know what is going on here and he was covered with blood. I thought I had better start talking to him before he starts attacking somebody else. Okay, I thought obviously he was a bit excited, so I thought the thing was just to talk to him. I thought these people usually have a message so I said 'what do you want?'"

"We want to start a war," one of the men told her. "I will shoot the police when they come. I want to kill them." Looking both men

     WHAT TO DO WHEN **LEADERSHIP** IS NEEDED

straight in the eye, she replied calmly: "That's not going to happen. I am here and I am going to listen to you."

"Would you like to give me what you have in your hands?" she continued.

As she waited for the police to arrive, Mrs. Loyau-Kennett continued to converse with both suspects for more than eight minutes without any harm coming to herself.

Some have labelled Loyau-Kennett a hero. Others, including some of her family who obviously although very proud of her actions, have said that it was very "foolhardy".

Her heroism is the point of many discussions, the real question, is how and why did she survive in such a crucial situation?

Now, I've no idea whether Mrs Loyau-Kennett has studied listening or undertaken any critical communication training (perhaps she has as she is a Cub Scout Mistress).

However, I do know that the communication principles she used were exactly right for handling difficult situations. And despite some of the difficult situations we managers face, you can't get any more difficult than one that could threaten your life.

So what are the skills Ingrid Loyau-Kennett used? Can you pick them?

Firstly, she took a non-threatening stance. Although she looked the principal protagonist in the eyes, she stood slightly angled to him with her hands in her pockets. Whilst not subservient, neither was she a threat to him.

Then she engaged him in the conversation. "What do you want?" Instead of threatening him, or saying something silly like "Why did you do that?", she got to the heart of what he wanted – attention to his cause.

Notice too that she was not agreeing with him nor highlighting his cause, she was merely asking "What do you want?"

Then when he answered, "We want to start a war," one of the men told her. "I will shoot the police when they come, I want to kill them" her communication skills really shone through.

She both listened attentively and stood her ground. Looking both men straight in the eye, she replied calmly: "That's not going to happen. I am here and I am going to listen to you."

Throughout the short but intense conversation, Loyau-Kennett's body language spoke of calmness. There were no hand gestures (either in an attempt to calm or otherwise) and her words were carefully chosen, e.g. "weapons" were never mentioned as she said "Would you like to give me what you have in your hands?"

As managers, I trust that the heroic action of Ingrid Loyau-Kennett will live long in your memory, particularly when faced with that difficult or stressful conversation you find yourself in.

Here are some thought starters to improve listening skills, starting with Loyau-Kennett's three, and one of my own:

1. Take a non-threatening stance: Particularly important if the team member seems upset. If possible sit down and ask them to join you. This demonstrates your interest as well as getting them to take some immediate action and thus lessens the threatening nature of standing.

2. Engage the person in the conversation: Ask non-threatening, generally open-ended questions, and one of the best can be "Tell me more …?" or "Can you give me an example of that?"

3. Listen attentively: You can even use words such as "I'm listening, please tell me more".

4. Finally, ask the person both how they feel about a certain situation and what they think about it: Using the word "feel" (e.g. "How do you feel about …?") gets them talking about their emotions, motivations, concerns, issues and so on, i.e. what we can't see from the outside. Using the word "think" (e.g. "What do you think about …?") gets them talking about the facts, logic, reasons and their perceptions of reality. Notice that the feel

     WHAT TO DO WHEN LEADERSHIP IS NEEDED

question started with "How" and the think question started with "What" thus reinforcing the feeling or thinking responses from the team member.

Now, if that's piqued your interest in improving your listening skills, here are a few statistics that will really make you think about the importance of effective listening. It's been said that:

- 85% of what we know we have learned through listening.
- People generally listen at a 25% comprehension rate.
- In a typical business day, we spend 45% of our time listening, 30% of our time talking, 16% reading and 9% writing.
- Less than 2% of all professionals have had formal education or learning to understand and improve listening skills and techniques.

And as the famous management guru Peter Drucker once said, "The most important thing in communication is hearing what isn't said". One can only do that through really listening.

Author's note

Some years ago I was called in to do some coaching with the GM of a manufacturing plant (approx., 200 employees). Although the operation was running well and profitably (it was the subsidiary of a multi-national firm), the GM's boss said that he was concerned with the reasonably high turnover in the GM's top team.

Sitting in on the GM's management meeting, then following him around the factory as he did his Monday morning walk through the plant, I noticed that all of his conversations were about facts – reason and logic. There was very little emotional sentiment, passion or excitement, and certainly no humour in the meeting and conversations with the various team leaders and workers.

My suggestion to the GM was, next Monday when he did his rounds to change one word in his conversations – change "think" to "feel", so instead of saying "What do you think about progress on the XYZ project?", say "How do you feel about progress on the XYZ project?"

The following Monday around lunch time, the GM rang me, very excitedly, saying "Bob, that was amazing. I have learnt so much more today about what's happening in the plant than ever before. People were telling me about their motivation, concerns, tensions, excitement – Wow!". The power of words!

Personal leadership review and learning

1. What words or phrases have you noticed that work for you in being a good listener? Why?

2. What other tactics or strategies do you see or hear that encourage the other person to speak both about their feelings and the facts around the situation?

3. What can I (or my organisation, my team) do differently (or keep doing) to improve the words we use with one another, and particularly in meetings to encourage more (or better) listening. For instance:
    *   What should I do more of?
    *   What should I do less of?
    *   What should I keep doing?

4. Is there something I now need to plan for as a result of this learning? If so, what?

Team Learning Exercise

This is an important team meeting and probably one that the team has not experienced or discussed before. Running a meeting on this subject, could well demonstrate to your team that you are, or working towards being, an empathic leader, prepared to listen to the thoughts and feelings of the team members.

1. Have team members read this chapter and ask them to draw up a list of words / phrases / questions they hear or use regularly that encourage people to talk openly.

2. At the start of the meeting, split team into pairs. Each pair is to share their list of items, then decide on three (only) that are they believe are the most effective.

    WHAT TO DO WHEN LEADERSHIP IS NEEDED

3. Have pairs share with the main team, their chosen items.

4. Lead a discussion with the aim of drawing up a list of actions that will improve communication within the team.

5. Conclude with a discussion on:
    - What should we do more of?
    - What should we do less of?
    - What should we keep doing?

Further suggested reading

Nicholls, N.P. *The Lost Art of Listening, Second Edition: How Learning to Listen Can Improve Relationships,* The Guilford Press, 2009.

Points to add to my Leadership Plan at the back of the book:

DEVELOP *SELF-LEADERSHIP* WITHIN YOURSELF AND YOUR TEAM

26. MULTITASKING, MARIJUANA, MANAGING?

- How to improve our ability to focus on key tasks

27. THE DEATH OF THE BLACKBERRY - WHAT'S IT GOT TO DO WITH COVID 19?

- How to decide the most appropriate working arrangements for the team and individual team members

STORY 26:
15 MAY 2015

Multitasking, Marijuana, Managing?

When we talk about multitasking, we are really talking about attention: the art of paying attention, the ability to shift our attention and more broadly, to exercise judgment about what objects are worthy of our attention. In fact despite its sophistication, the brain can only concentrate on one task at a time.

Chapter Objectives

- To improve our task completion and get more things done.

Chapter theme

In today's fast moving world we seem to do many things at once. For instance, as you read this chapter you may also be texting a friend or colleague, talking on the phone, or even checking emails on your phone. You must be a true multitasker!

Multitasking, Marijuana, Managing?

How's your "To Do" list progressing today?

"To Do" list, you might say, surely that's old technology?

Yes, it is. However, the result of research suggests it might be time to give the old "To Do" list a comeback opportunity. You may recall (and for those still using them) that the fundamental principle behind "To Do" lists, is that you prioritise the list of tasks, then work on each one until the list is complete. Focus, concentration and one task at a time, are the cornerstones of a good "To Do" list proponent.

By comparison, in today's fast moving world we seem to do many things at once. For instance, as you read this article you may also be texting a friend or colleague, talking on the phone, or even checking emails on your phone. A true multitasker!

If this describes you, the latest findings may come as a shock. Scientists at Stanford University have found that people who multitask are far less effective than those who concentrate on one thing at a time. Professor Clifford I. Nass, one of the study team, put it this way, "Multitaskers were just lousy at everything." So, when you multitask, it seems as if you're doing a lot of work, but you're not doing most (or any) of it well.

However, multitasking in fact is a misnomer. When we talk about multitasking, we are really talking about attention: the art of paying attention, the ability to shift our attention and more broadly, to exercise judgment about what objects are worthy of our attention. In fact despite its sophistication, the brain can only concentrate on one task at a time. Edward Hallowell, psychiatrist and author of CrazyBusy describes multitasking as, "a mythical activity in which people believe they can perform two or more tasks simultaneously."

Because the brain can only focus on one thing at a time, so-called "multitasking" forces the brain to take shorter and shorter time on unlike tasks, thus reducing our effectiveness.

　　　WHAT TO DO WHEN LEADERSHIP IS NEEDED

Multitasking may even be affecting how we plan our work. Frank Patrick of consulting firm Focused Performance, suggests that when it comes to say, working on two projects at the same time, "many of our project plans could very well be twice as long as they need to be." He further suggests that multitasking may well start from the allocation of resources to projects, "The idea of assigning half or a quarter of one head count to a project is a good way to start down the slippery slope of multitasking."

Studies at the University of Michigan confirm Patrick's assertions. They go further to say that, "People lose time when they have to switch from one task to another and the amount of time lost increases with the complexity of the tasks."

In addition to reduced effectiveness, there may also be other downsides to multitasking. A study conducted at the Institute of Psychiatry, University of London by Dr. Glenn Wilson way back in 2005, found that "Those distracted by incoming email and phone calls saw a 10-point fall in their IQ - more than twice that found in studies of the impact of smoking marijuana." Wilson went on to say that, "Those who are constantly breaking away from tasks to react to email or text messages suffer similar effects on the mind as losing a night's sleep."

Now, there have been many technological advances since 2005 that have allowed us to "multitask" more. I wonder what that has done to our IQ?

What's the message here for managers?

- It's not only legitimate, but highly productive if people turn off all electronic devices during meetings, so that they can concentrate on what needs to be achieved. Your introductory words could be something like, "Who'd like to reduce their IQ by 10%?"

- It would seem that the time honoured time-management technique of putting like- tasks together, prioritising and taking one task at a time, has a proven basis in scientific research. Time to start the "To Do" list again?

- Perhaps encouraging your people to do things such as their emails in specific blocks of time might be an option. One manager I know recently reached an agreement with his boss – they agreed to answer emails by 10am each morning – if anything else came up during the day that was urgent, they would phone, not text nor email.

- Give people the opportunity to "check out" from constant media input such as phone, text, email, and more recently digital messaging – particularly out of office hours.

- Think about the allocation of resources, particularly to projects – is this likely to affect the performance of your people? How could these resources be better allocated to allow people to focus?

- Then of course, there's the open-plan office – so essential to the economic well-being of the organisation and so useful for staff interaction (?). Perhaps making people aware of the downsides of multitasking and discussing alternative strategies in staff meetings, might be a start.

- Finally, there's the great feeling of satisfaction one gets from completing a task. Salespeople, and sales managers in particular, have traditionally been very good at recognising and appreciating results - both theirs and their people. How could you encourage recognition and appreciation of completed tasks with your people?

No doubt as you've read this article, you've thought of some other things that might reduce both yours and your peoples' dependence on multitasking. As for me? I can now tick "article on multitasking" off my 'To Do' list. Now to the next one . . .

Personal leadership review and learning

1. When was the last time you drew up a "To Do" list? Would it be useful? Where would you write or place it for best effect?

2. At a personal level, when do you find yourself most frustrated with not achieving the things that you want to do during the day? What causes this frustration?

     WHAT TO DO WHEN LEADERSHIP IS NEEDED

3. What can I (or my organisation, my team) do differently (or keep doing) to improve the achievement of our key tasks? For instance:
    - What should I do more of?
    - What should I do less of?
    - What should I keep doing?

4. Is there something I now need to plan for as a result of this learning? If so, what?

Team Learning Exercise

This story is principally aimed at improving your own time efficiency and effectiveness. However, if you see that it could also benefit some of your team, the following team exercise may be useful.

1. Distribute the story prior to your meeting and ask everyone to read and answer the following questions (as usual, feel free to pick and choose the questions).
    - What techniques do you use to make your day more productive?
    - As a team member:
        » How or what can I do that would make life a little easier for other team members?
        » What could other team members do for me that would help my day be more productive?

2. At the meeting ask team members to contribute to the discussion the:
    - Things I can do to help other team members perform at their best.
    - Things that other team members can do that would help me perform at my best.

3. Lead a discussion on the selected suggestions to reach consensus on:
    - What action needs to be taken?
    - By whom?
    - By when?
    - How will our results be measured? When?

Further suggested reading

Hallowell, E. "CrazyBuzy", Penguin Random House, 2007.

Nass, C. (2013), "The Myth of Multitasking" https://www.bradford.ac.uk/library/

Knight, W. (2005) "Info-Mania dents IQ more than marijuana" New Scientist.
https://www.newscientist.com/article/dn7298-info-mania-dents-iq-more-than- marijuana/

Hari, J. "Stolen Focus: Why you can't pay attention". Bloomsbury Publishing, Dublin 2002.

Points to add to my Leadership Plan at the back of the book:

STORY 27:
25 FEB 2022

The Death of the Blackberry - What's it got to do with Covid 19?

With the changes to workplace practices (some have actually disappeared!), how is your organisation managing this "new normal"? And importantly, how are their efforts succeeding or otherwise for you and your team?

Chapter Objectives

- To decide the most appropriate working arrangements for the team and individual team members.

Chapter theme

With the changes in the way we work brought about by Covid 19, for example through lockdowns, social distancing and working from home, what's the impact on individuals, teams, productivity, motivation, team-work, and even corporate culture? How do managers and teams address the 'new normal'?

The Death of the Blackberry

In January 2022, the Blackberry, the iconic phone of the early 2000's and the item that first allowed us to send and receive emails on our phones (incidentally, about five years before Apple and Samsung did so), ceased to operate. The company is no longer supporting the phones, so they may now have become a nostalgic paperweight (for those "lucky" enough to have had one – they were very expensive and often provided by one's employer – I wasn't that lucky!).

Now, you may be thinking, what's the link between the iconic Blackberry phone and the Covid pandemic?

Very simple.

BlackBerry kicked off the technological blurring of personal time and office time that these days — with every device capable of connecting us to our colleagues and everyone else — is practically complete.

Who amongst us has not sent or received a text, email or other message electronically outside of what used to be called "normal office hours"? And how about electronic meetings, such as Zoom? For those reading this who are old enough to remember, it's only been a little over 30 years since we were (safely) able to 'sign-off' at the end of the working day.

The Covid pandemic, and the resultant actions of governments around the world, have in recent times placed an embargo on us meeting together and have perhaps inadvertently accelerated this blurring of personal and office time. The majority of business communication now is via email, text, Skype, Zoom or some other technological form of communication. Face to face meetings within offices and within what used to be "office time", are almost a thing of the past.

And now as we move into the "new normal", many organisations and managers are struggling to deal and manage with this changing nature of work – often to the detriment of their employees, through such things as micro-managing, over-supervising or perhaps even worse, under-managing. Others have seen the positives and have

 WHAT TO DO WHEN LEADERSHIP IS NEEDED

found a new and revitalised outlook on the nature of work, for example, where, when and how it should be done.

As you read this story, many of you will have experienced a work from home period or perhaps even a hybrid home/office period. Much has already been written and studied on the plusses and minuses of these workplace changes.

However, the jury is still out on a raft of the results. For example: Is the new form of work more or less productive? Is it better or worse for staff morale, motivation and engagement? Does it help or hinder the development of 'team', or even, 'organisation culture'?

And are such things as long established power balances now shifting requiring new boundaries and psychological contracts to be considered and negotiated?

No doubt you'll have your own views on these and other questions. However, for managers, this new normal can be a really tough gig!

One company, the $80 billion, Sydney based tech giant Atlassian, has met this leadership challenge head on. At its recent annual conference, it announced that under its new "Team Anywhere" policy, the company's 5,700 global staff will be allowed to work from anywhere as long as the company has a base there, they have a legal right to work there, and the time zone is broadly aligned with the rest of their team. Remarkably, employees will be expected to come into the office only four times a year, though interestingly, most have said they still plan to attend in person at least 50% of the time.

"Talent still exists anywhere it just doesn't happen to need to exist within 50 kilometres of an existing office," Atlassian co-founder and Co-CEO, Scott Farquhar said. "If you want to have an office environment you can do that", Farquhar said of how the new arrangement will work, and added "the policy will stipulate that you're not allowed to have meetings with only some of your co-workers, if one person is on Zoom everyone's on Zoom individually."

This surely represents Atlassian's commitment to remote work well after the pandemic demands it.

And another company, Perpetual Guardian, a New Zealand based trust company, through forward thinking leadership has been addressing the "work from home/work in the office" question since 2018 – long before Covid hit. Perpetual Guardian has now taken a different approach and made the four-day week a standard part of the way it works.

The basis behind Perpetual Guardian's four-day week is to:

- Encourage staff to consider how they can organise time off within teams while still meeting customer and business imperatives.

- Give employees sufficient time to think about how they can work differently, and encourage them to come up with their own measure of productivity.

Andrew Barnes, who is also Perpetual Guardian's founder, says "the four-day week is not just having a day off a week – it's about delivering productivity, and meeting customer service standards, meeting personal and team business goals and objectives."

Perpetual Guardian tested their assumptions about productivity through a company-wide trial, the results of which made headlines around the world. As Barnes commented, "the rise of the gig economy represents a new industrial era, and we have not had a conversation about its implications for our economy and society".

And the results for Perpetual Guardian? The company claimed productivity increased by 20 per cent during the trial, and staff were more engaged and enthusiastic.

And here's the kicker - Perpetual Guardian which has more than 240 employees spread across the country - made the four-day week not compulsory, but an option for all its full-time workers!

These are but two examples of organisations that have approached the question of why, how, where and when, work is done, in quite different ways.

How is your organisation managing this "new normal"? And importantly, how are their efforts succeeding for you and your team?

Personal leadership review and learning

1. What's going well or not so well in these two stories?

2. At a personal level, what are the leadership lessons you can draw from this chapter? For example;
    - How clear are you on your organisation's intentions with remote, hybrid, or pre-existing working arrangements?

3. What should I (or my organization, my team) do differently now?
    - Do I need to take any action regarding working arrangements? Why/Why not?

4. Is there something I now need to plan for as a result of this learning? If so, what?
    - In particular, do you believe there is scope for changes in the way work is managed in your organisation, i.e., Why? Where? When? How?

Author's note

A recent study has found we may be suffering from excessive stress and anxiety about work expectations even if we don't actively check work emails in our off-work hours. The mere expectation of being in contact 24/7 is enough to increase strain for employees and their families, the research suggests.

In today's ultra-connected world, with many people often getting work emails sent to their smartphones, a growing number of countries and companies are endorsing "right to disconnect" laws, recreating a much-needed boundary between work and home.

As I wrote this chapter, a number of countries have, or are considering introducing these, "right to disconnect" laws that stipulate, "If?", "When?" and sometimes, "How?" employees are able to be contacted outside normal working hours.

For example, Portugal has made it illegal for employees to be texted after hours, although firms with less than 10 employees are exempt.

Belgium has taken a slightly different approach starting with Civil Servants who will have, "the legal right to ignore calls from their employers outside office hours".

France, in particular, has been ahead of the world in establishing legal frameworks protecting a person's right to disconnect. Back in 2001 the idea was first floated when the French Supreme Court ruled that employees are under no obligation to bring work home, and as technology progressed the Court continued to update its ruling. In 2004, for example, it was established that it was not misconduct if an employee was not reachable on a smartphone outside of work hours.

The right to disconnect was solidified at the beginning of 2017 with France introducing the El Khomri law, which suggests every employee contract must include a negotiation of obligations required of an employee regarding how connected they are outside of office hours. The law is reasonably vague and doesn't restrict after-hours work communication, but rather obliges organisations to negotiate these terms clearly with prospective employees. At the moment, the law only applies to organisations of 100 or more employees.

Italy has also recently incorporated a very similar right to disconnect law, again simply requiring contractual clarity over an employee's responsibility to communicate outside of general work hours.

What's the legal situation in your country? Importantly, what's the "unwritten expectation" in your organisation, and perhaps in your industry?

Team Learning Exercise

There are lots of thought starters and questions for both teams and team members within this story. And if you and your organisation are working remotely, hybrid, or in a "suspended zone" at the moment, due to external pressures such as Covid restrictions or maybe pro-actively such as Atlassian and Perpetual Guardian, you may have to be quite creative in the way in which you use these stories with your team.

Here's a suggested way you might use it with your team.

　　　WHAT TO DO WHEN **LEADERSHIP** IS NEEDED

1. Distribute the "Death of the Blackberry" story prior to a team meeting and ask everyone to read and answer the following questions (Feel free to pick and choose the questions, or add your own:

    - Why do you believe Blackberry (which at the time was hugely expensive by comparison to a normal cell or mobile phone) was made so readily available to employees – in many cases, provided free?
    - How can we as a team manage our time more efficiently and effectively while still meeting customer and business imperatives?
    - If we decide that we can work differently, how do we ensure productivity is measured and maintained?
    - What might be the next potential steps in changing the way we work together? What help do we need from each other, our managers, our organisation?
    - Should we have an embargo on 'out of hours' communication? Why/Why not?

2. At the meeting ask team members to contribute to the discussion the:
    - Things I can do to help other team members perform at their best during this new normal.
    - Things that other team members can do that would help me perform at my best.

3. Lead a discussion on the selected suggestions to reach consensus on:
    - What action needs to be taken?
    - By whom?
    - By when?
    - How will our results be measured? When?

Further suggested reading

Haas, M. *"5 Challenges of Hybrid Work – and How to Overcome Them"*, https://hbr.org/2022/02/5-challenges-of-hybrid-work-and-how-to-overcome-them

Ashton, J. *The New Normal: A Roadmap to Resilience in the Pandemic Era,* William Morrow, 2021.

Points to add to my Leadership Plan at the back of the book

CONCLUSION – MANAGER OR LEADER?

I started this book with the story of the little girl on the plane asking her mother whether the Business Class people (behind the curtain) were learners and how that piqued my interest in whether leaders are born or could one learn to become a leader?

Maybe you've come to your own conclusion or have some thoughts on which is the case as you've read the stories and perhaps used some of the personal and team learning exercises. One of my intentions for the book, is to have you identify the things you do well when managing or influencing others, and how these skills and characteristics can lead to your further development as a leader. That still doesn't answer the question of course, but probably tips the scales slightly in favour of the nurture side of the debate.

Another short story on how I got the idea of writing What To Do When Leadership Is Needed, and which also happens to explain the underpinnings of the book, may well give you a clue to my position on the debate, and could also be useful to crystalise the distinction between management and leadership.

The idea came to me over a decade ago when launching the Chinese version of my first book, What To Do When You Become The Boss, in Beijing. I was asked to give a talk at the Beijing Institute of Technology to the Marketing students. Being briefed that only about 20 per cent of the students spoke English, I would be provided with an interpreter. So, I used a lot of visual aids and some good (hopefully) humour.

One of my aids, was a 'hat', which I called the "Manager's Hat" as an analogy, that people get when they are appointed into a managerial role. And people will do things for you because of the manager's hat that you wear.

However, it's only when you take that hat off, or for example have it taken away by an organisational change such as a move to self-managed teams, that you discover whether you are a leader or not.

The question I ask is "Would these people still do the things you ask of them, even though you are not now formally their manager?" If the answer is an unequivocal "Yes", then you know you've earned a leadership badge (which I then proudly stuck on my chest).

My interpreter, whom I found out later was a senior lecturer at the Institute, said that the distinction between management and leadership was the best she has heard and really appreciated by the students. So, point made.

As readers of the book, my question for you now to consider is "Would your people still do the things you ask of them, even if you were formally not their manager?"

LEADING & MANAGING FOR RESULTS

My Personal Leadership Plan - Taking an active role in my future development

Name:

As you read through What To Do When Leadership Is Needed, I asked you to focus on developing new management skills, polishing existing ones and providing plenty of time for reflection on what it takes to be a good manager, and ultimately, an effective leader.

The final part in the work of What To Do When Leadership Is Needed, is therefore a focus on leadership. This plan aims to provide the opportunity for you to take the next step along your leadership development pathway.

By working your way through the questions posed, my hope is that you will have a template that you can use not only now, but to which you can return over many years to come.

All the best with your leadership development.

Bob Selden

This plan involves four sections and concludes with your own one-page leadership template.

Section 1: My Strengths, Under-Developed Talents and Blind Spots.
- What have I learnt about myself during this learning process?

Section 2: My Role and Career Success.
- How does my profile fit with my career success?

Section 3: Developing into My Role as a Leader.
- What do I need to do to take the next steps?

Section 4: Leaders leave legacies. What will mine be?
- How will people describe me as a leader?

Finally, my one-page Template for Leadership Success.
- My plan for now and for my future!

Section 1:
My Strengths, Under-Developed Talents and Blind Spots

As part of reading the stories in "What To Do When Leadership Is Needed" you will have most likely jotted down some pertinent learning points in some of the following areas:

- The Importance of STRUCTURE and ROLES in developing leadership
- Setting a STRATEGY for leadership
- How to prepare for the inevitable CRISIS as a leader
- Developing PERSONAL LEADERSHIP
- Developing TRUST and CREDIBILITY
- Managing STAKEHOLDERS
- Building a TEAM or a GROUP
- The leadership aspects of PEOPLE MANAGEMENT
- Motivating people through PERFORMANCE MANAGEMENT
- Leading your people to provide CUSTOMER SERVICE
- Developing CREATIVITY within your people
- COMMUNICATING to INFLUENCE
- SELF–MANAGEMENT

Please review some of the above (as you feel necessary), then answer the following questions.

1.1. What are the three key strengths that I bring to the role of leader?

1.2. What are the areas where I believe I can still develop further as a leader? Please list three:

1.3. What do I consider to be my blind spots? These are aspects of management / leadership that you least prefer or with which you are least comfortable. (Note: You may be able to do these quite well when pushed, you just don't like doing them!).

Section 2:
My Role and Career Success

During your career, you've probably worked with a number of managers – some of whom you consider to be good or even excellent, leaders.

2.1. Think about these people, particularly those that you and others consider to be very successful in their role. What makes them successful in their role? (We've listed some headings as thought starters – if these are appropriate, jot down some reasons why your successful people are good at these – or change/add as many headings as you feel appropriate and say why):

- Technical expertise – Why?

- Length of time in the company/organisation – Why?

- Personality – Why?

- Ability to have a good balance between Leading, Managing and Operating – Why?

- Expertise at managing-up – Why?

- Management style – Why?

- Others that are relevant to me ... Why?

- Others... Why?

2.2. How well do my strengths and under-developed talents measure up with the above?

- Good fit with:

- Questionable fit with:

Section 3:
Developing into My Role as a Leader

3.1. What coaching, mentoring, training or development activities have you implemented for or with your people and/or peers over the last 12 months?

3.2. What success have you had with these? What's been the impact:

- on you?

- on others?

3.3. What feedback have you sought or received from others?

3.4. If you've not received any feedback, what do you now need to do
to get that feedback?

3.5. What new or additional networking opportunities have you
availed yourself of since reading "What To Do When Leadership
Is Needed"? (these would be outside your team)

Section 4:
Leaders leave legacies. What will mine be?

4.1. Assume it is three years from now. You have just moved on from your current role. How would people (such as peers, team members, direct reports, managers, customers, suppliers etc.) describe you if someone asked . . .

"What was..............................(put your name here) like?"

Rather than just write a list of adjectives, or throwaway phrases such as "He/she was a good manager", please be as descriptive as possible. Try to write a number of sentences that specifically describe (behaviours, observable characteristics) the person (you) who has just left. To make this as realistic as possible, please write your first name in front of each statement, then complete the sentence:

was someone who . . .

was someone who . . .

was someone who . . .

was someone who . . .

Before proceeding to the Leadership Plan on the following page, please review Sections 1 to 4. What are the two or three things that stand out for you? In particular, you should ask, have I been able to develop with my people . . .
- a shared understanding of *the environment?*
- a shared *vision* of where we are going?
- a shared set of *organisational values?*
- a shared *feeling of power?*

My Leadership Plan

I now see **myself as a leader** who (this should be a summary of your reflections on Sections 1 to 4 and what you intend doing) . . .

The **challenges** I face to fully develop my leadership capabilities are:

I may need help for my further development such as:

The **people I intend to involve** in my leadership development are:

I have specifically set aside ...... hours on   /   /   at............
to reflect and review my progress.

REFERENCES

Introduction

Smith, P. Lead with a Story, American Management Association, New York, 2012.

Vroom, V.H. & Yetton, P.W., Leadership and Decision Making, University of Pittsburgh Press, 1973.

Story 1

Birkman, C. *3 Crucial Steps to Create Role Clarity Within Your Team. Perception Connections;* the Birkman blog on perception, personality and organizational success. https://blog.birkman.com/3-steps-to-create-role-clarity-within-your-team.

Selden, B, What To Do When You Become The Boss: How new managers become successful managers, Hachette, 2011 (revised edition 2015).

Story 2

Einhorn, D. Fooling Some of the People All of the Time, A Long Short (and Now Complete) Story, Updated with New Epilogue. Wiley 2010.

Goffee, R. & Jones, G. Why Should Anyone Be Led by You? Harvard Business School Press 2006.

Story 3

Finkelstein, S., Whitehead, A., & Campbell, J., Think Again: Why Good Leaders Make Bad Decisions and How to Keep it From Happening to You, McGraw-Hill 2009.

Story 4

Benns, M. The Men Who Killed Qantas, Random House Australia, 2010.

Collins, J.C. & Porras, J.L., Built to Last, Harper Business, 2004.

De Geus, A. P., The Living Company, Harvard Business Review Press, 2002. Siddiqui, M. Leading from the Heart, Sage Publications Pvt. Ltd, 2014.

Story 5

Gitomer, J. Customer Satisfaction Is Worthless, Customer Loyalty Is Priceless: How to Make Customers Love You, Keep Them Coming Back and Tell Everyone They Know. Bard Press, 1998.

Griffin, J. Customer Loyalty: How to Earn It, How to Keep It, Wiley, 1995.

Story 6

Jordan-Meier, J., The Four Stages of Highly Effective Crisis Management, Boca Raton, FL : CRS Press, 2011.

Story 7

Ackerman, B. *You Had Me at "I'm Sorry": The Impact of Physicians' Apologies on Medical Malpractice Litigation,* Healthcare Medical Malpractice, November 6, 2018.

Cahill, L. *How To Say Sorry,* NZ Privacy Commissioner, 13 February 2017,
https://privacy.org.nz/blog/how-to-say-sorry/

Robbennolt, J.K., *Apologies and Medical Error,* Journal of Clinical Orthopaedics and Related Research, 2009, Feb., 467 (2), 376-382

Story 8

Erickson T., *Leading from the Base of the Beanstalk,* Harvard Business Review, 21 May 2010.

Story 9

Covey, S.M.R., *How the Best Leaders Build Trust,* Leadership Now,
https://www.leadershipnow.com/CoveyOnTrust.html

Jacobs, C.N., *Ineffective-Leader-Induced Occupational Stress,* SAGE Open,
https://journals.sagepub.com/doi/10.1177/2158244019855858

Ray, B., *Who's afraid of the big bad boss?,* Florida State University, FSU News,
https://www.fsu.edu/news/2006/12/04/bad.boss/

Story 10

Herzberg's Motivation Theory, Expert Program Management, https://expertprogrammanagement.com/2018/04/herzbergs-two-factor-theory/

Muth, M. & Selden, B., Setting the Tone from the Top: How director conversations shape culture, AICD, 2017.

Story 11

Covey, S., Seven Habits of Highly Effective People, Free Press 2004.

Luhmann, N., Trust and Power, Wiley, 2017.

Story 12

Ratan Tata – *Indian Businessman* https://www.britannica.com/biography/Ratan-Tata

Story 13

Selden, B., What To Do When You Become The Boss: How new managers become successful managers, Hachette, Sydney, 201 0.

Story 14

Kurtzman, K., *An interview with Charles Handy,* Strategy + Business, https://www.strategy-business.com/article/12188.

Ribeiro, S., *Workplace Collaboration: Team vs Group,* Flockblog https://blog.flock.com/workplace-collaboration-teams-vs-groups, May 1, 2020.

Story 15

Erickson, T. *Leading from the Base of the Beanstalk,* Harvard Business Review, 21 May 2010.

New Zealand Work Research Institute, *Understanding the needs of New Zealand's ageing workforce,* https://workresearch.aut.ac.nz/ data/ assets/pdf_file/0005/378932/2015- Understanding-Ageing-Workforce-report,-FOW.pdf, August 2015.

Story 16

Harris, C., *Working from home is more complicated than we thought.*
Stuff, Jan 17, 2021. https://www.stuff.co.nz/business/123891998/
working-from-home-is-more- complicated-than-we-thought

Employee Engagement Has Fallen While Working From Home, Consultancy.
com.au, 18 July 2021
https://www.consultancy.com.au/news/3656/employee-engagement-
has- fallen-while-working-from-home

Story 17

Mumford, T.V., Campion, M.A., & Morgeson, F.P., *The leadership skills
strataplex: Leadership skill requirements across organizational levels,*
The Leadership Quarterly, Vol 18 No. 2, 2007.

Prince, E.T., *Business acumen: a critical concern of modern
leadership development: Global trends accelerate the move away
from traditional approaches.* Human Resource Management
International Digest, https://www.emerald.com/insight/content/
doi/10.1108/09670730810900811/full/h tml

Story 18

Bell, M.F., By Carrot or by Stick?, Tillamook Headlight Herald, Jun 27,
2012, https://www.tillamookheadlightherald.com/news/by-carrot-
or-by-stick/article_397b7264-c085-11e1-80e0-001a4bcf887a.html

Employee Engagement 2011/2012 Report, Kenexa® High Performance
Institute, http://www.repman.com.tr/en/2012/08/employee-
engagement-20112012-report-kenexa-high-performance-institute/

Herzberg, F., *One More Time: How Do You Motivate Employees?,*
Harvard Business Review, January–February 1968.

Story 19

Cadieux, M., *3 Easy Steps to Give Powerful Employee Recognition,*
Applauz Blog,
https://www.applauz.me/resources/how-to-give-employee-
recognition

Story 20

Zenger, J. *The 6 Vital Elements Of Effective Performance Management Systems,* Forbes Feb 16, 2017, https://www.forbes.com/sites/jackzenger/2017/02/16/the-6-vital-elements-of-effective-performance-management-systems/?sh=311553fb618e

Story 21

Griffin, D and Bronstein, S. *FAA inspectors: Southwest tried to hide safety problems,* CNN April 3, 2008. http://edition.cnn.com/2008/US/04/02/southwest.faa.inspection/ (accessed Lindahl, L. quoted in, Comparing the Perspectives of Managers and Employees of Teaching Hospitals

Fear and flying and the pathetic FAA, New York Times, April 11, 2008 https://www.nytimes.com/2008/04/11/opinion/11iht-edfaa.1.11908731.html

Story 22

Hyken, S. The Cult of the Customer: Create an Amazing Customer Experience that Turns Satisfied Customers into Customer, Sound Wisdom 2020.

Levitt, T. *What business are you in? Classic advice from Theodore Levitt,* Harvard Business Review, https://hbr.org/2006/10/what-business-are-you-in-classic-advice-from-theodore-levitt

Story 23

Appleton, R. *N.L. Jones, South Dallas man famed for artful birdhouses crafted from scrap items, dies at 82,* Dallas News, March 2012 https://www.dallasnews.com/obituaries/obituaries/2012/03/09/n.l.-jones-south-dallas-man-famed-for-artful-birdhouses-crafted-from-scrap-items-dies-at-82

Chak-keung Wong, S. & Ladkin, A., *Exploring the relationship between employee creativity and job-related motivators in the Hong Kong hotel industry,* International Journal of Hospitality Management 27 (2008) 426–437.

De Bono, E. Six Thinking Hats, Little Brown and Company, 1985.

Dougherty, D. & Hardy, C., *Sustained Product Innovation in Large, Mature Organizations,* Academy of Management, Vol 39, Issue 5, Oct., 1996.

Mohebbifar, R., Zakaria Kiaei, M., Khosravizadeh, O. & Mohseni, M., *About Job Motivation,* Global Journal Of Health Science, 2014 Nov; 6(6): 112–118.

National survey commissioned by FCEDA points to "creativity gap" in U.S. workplace, Businesswire, December 19, 2014, https://www.businesswire.com/news/home/20141219005600/en/National-survey-commissioned-by-FCEDA-points-to-%E2%80%9Ccreativity-gap%E2%80%9D-in-U.S.-workplace

Story 24

Berger, J., *Arousal Increases Social Transmission of Information,* Short Report, The Association for Psychological Science, 18 Apr 2011.

Boyle, S. *I Dreamed A Dream,* https://www.youtube.com/watch?v=yE1Lxw5ZyXk

Carroll, D. *United Breaks Guitars,* https://www.youtube.com/watch?v=5YGc4zOqozo

Carroll, D. *United Breaks Guitars 4.* Dave Carroll Responds to Customer Service incident on United Flight 3411 https://www.youtube.com/watch?v=yQz8qqioCt8

Story 25

Llipos, G., *6 Ways Effective Listening Can Make You A Better Leader,* Forbes, May 20, 2013.

Story 26

Gorlick, A., *Media multitaskers pay mental price, Stanford study shows,* Stanford News, Aug 24, 2009.

Story 27

Multitasking undermines our efficiency, study suggests, American Phycological Society, October 2001, Vol 32, No. 9.

O'Connor, T., *Are distractions making you underperform?* https://www.lawsociety.com.au/resources/resources/career-hub/are-distractions-making-you-underperform

Stothart, C., Mitchum, A., &, Yehnert, C., *The attentional cost of receiving a cell phone notification,* National Library of Medicine, Epub 2015 Jun 29, https://pubmed.ncbi.nlm.nih.gov/26121498